The Open University

hool

Book 1

What is a business?

*Written by Diane Preston with contributions
from Mick Fryer and George Watson*

The Open University Walton Hall, Milton Keynes MK7 6AA

First published 2006. Second edition 2007. Third edition 2010. Fourth edition 2011.

Edited and designed by The Open University.

Printed and bound in the United Kingdom by Charlesworth Press, Wakefield.

ISBN 978 1 8487 3586 6

4.1

Contents

Introduction to Book 1

Welcome to Book 1 of B120. Book 1 is the first of five B120 books, but there is another essential course component that you will use throughout B120, and it is to this that you should now turn. This is the B120 Study Companion. It will guide you through the books, making comments on the activities and showing you where to go for additional information, including online resources. The Study Companion will also enable you to chart your development and personal learning journey. If you are to get the most out of B120 and become an effective student, you should always have your Study Companion to hand. Please read the introduction to the Study Companion before you continue with Book 1.

All important terms in the B120 books are in **bold italics** the first time they are used. This indicates that they are defined in the glossary, and that you need to understand the meaning of the terms in order to proceed with your studies. The glossary for the course can be found on the B120 course website.

There are discussions in your tutor group forum (TGF) about specific issues in each B120 book. You are required to participate in these as they are designed to reinforce your understanding of the books. Details of the TGF and how to use it are provided in your Study Companion and the B120 Assignment Booklet.

Aims and objectives

The aims of Book 1 are to:

- describe some common characteristics of businesses;
- explore what makes businesses different from one another;
- understand the main sociological, technological, economic, environmental and political forces that impact on businesses;
- explain how organisational cultures emerge within businesses;
- outline different types of structures and how they might impact on how work is organised within a business;
- identify the importance of business ethics;
- provide an introduction to business functions.

Structure

Book 1 is divided into seven study sessions:

Session 1	provides an introduction to the question, 'what is a business?'
Session 2	describes the external environment within which businesses operate. Here we consider the sociological, technological, economic, environmental and political factors which impact on businesses.
Session 3	addresses the structure of businesses. It considers the question of why structure is important, and looks at different types of structures and at ways of analysing them. It also explores the distinction between formal and informal structures.
Session 4	shows how examining the culture of a business can help us to understand its less obvious features. It explores the significance of the theory of national culture and considers some of the factors that shape the culture of a business.
Session 5	discusses the question of how we ought to conduct business, that is, business ethics. It looks at how the values of people both within and outside a business can affect how business is conducted and explores some of the complexities of ethical decision making.
Session 6	provides an introduction to the different functions of business: human resource management, marketing, accounting and finance, operations and information management. It considers what these functions do and how they work together.
Session 7	focuses on small businesses and the type of entrepreneurial spirit and skills that constitute the basis of a business launch and developing success.

Session 1 What is business?

Why are we studying 'what is a business?'? 'Business' is hard to define for the very reason that there is so much of it around us, in all sorts of different shapes and sizes. It is clear that, while every business is different, there are common characteristics that we can use to identify a business. There are also some academic frameworks available to us to challenge our thinking about what a business might be.

It is important to question what a business is because people tend to think in terms of large, well-known, successful businesses, whereas business is, in fact, everywhere. Any typical high street will have banks, florists, hairdressers, newsagents, estate agents, cafés, and so on. Business is such an integral part of our lives that we do not normally stop to think about it. But, where does a business come from? How is it run? What makes it succeed? Why do people like to use it? This course aims to provide some answers to these types of questions.

You will all have participated in a business, as a consumer, as an employee or as a client. We are not assuming that you have direct business experience, or that you are currently working within a business. We have adopted the perspective of an interested onlooker, keen to understand more about business and some of the academic ideas and models that might develop that understanding. Business is everywhere! Let's take a look at some of its key aspects.

The **aims and objectives** of study Session 1 are to:

- begin to address the question, 'what is a business?';
- offer some definitions of 'business';
- explore some of the similarities and differences between businesses;
- outline Morgan's metaphor model, which helps us to see business from different points of view.

1.1 What a business does

One of the biggest problems we face as students of business is that 'business' may mean different things to different people. Even those working within the same business will have different perceptions and definitions of it. Moreover, one view is not necessarily better than another. Use Activity 1.1 to explore your understanding of what a business is and what it does.

Activity 1.1

Spend about **15 minutes** on this activity

Purpose: to identify some common characteristics of businesses.

Task: consider the list below and note any common characteristics that, for you, define them as businesses:

- a branch of a national bank
- an electricity supply company
- a school parent–teacher association
- a local medical centre
- a village post office
- a local car sales firm
- the United Nations
- a hairdresser.

Feedback

You may have started by thinking about some formal characteristics of businesses, such as whether they employ staff and keep accounts of income and expenditure. Here are the ones we thought of. You may have listed more.

- They consist of a number of people.
- The people who belong to them will probably share some values and views about the purpose(s) of the business.
- They will have some income and costs.
- They will need different types of resources to produce different types of goods or services.
- They are likely to need to co-ordinate a number of different activities undertaken by individuals.
- They are identifiable as different from other groups of people.

You may also have noted the common sense point: 'it's a business if most people think it is'.

Businesses enable objectives to be achieved that could not be achieved by the efforts of individuals on their own. Businesses come in all shapes and sizes, but have three factors in common: people, objectives and structure. It is the interaction of people to achieve objectives that forms the basis of a business, and some form of structure is needed within which people's interactions and efforts are focused. The direction and control of the interactions form the role of management. This sounds straightforward, but we have already identified that those who come together to form businesses, those who work in them and those who manage them may have different objectives, needs and understandings of the businesses. It is these types of issues which form the basis of studying business and, hence, much of the content of B120 and future courses in the BA in Business Studies programme.

Businesses are often differentiated in terms of the sector of the economy to which they belong: public or private.

The ***private sector*** comprises those businesses that are not controlled by the State.

The ***public sector*** comprises any part of the nation's economy that is controlled and operated by the State.

In this course we shall also refer to ***for profit*** or ***non-profit*** (sometimes called ***not-for-profit***) businesses. This differentiates businesses according to whether their primary motive is profit; that is, the enhancement of their owners' and certain ***stakeholders'*** wealth. It is possible to allocate most businesses into one or other of the quadrants shown in Table 1.1.

Table 1.1 Types of businesses

Public sector	Not for profit
local authorities, schools, government departments, hospitals, armed forces, state-owned enterprises, which in some countries include *public utilities*	*charities*, *voluntary organisations*, clubs and societies, *trade unions*, *pressure groups*, religious organisations
Private sector	**For profit**
sole traders, partnerships, producer and *consumer co-operatives*	railways, airlines, nationalised industries

You should make sure that you understand the terms that are highlighted in Table 1.1. The glossary is on the B120 course website.

In non-profit businesses the primary aims are expressed in terms other than financial profitability. This does not mean that the intention is to make a loss! Nor does it mean that losses can be the normal or predominant financial outcome for the business. Cash is as important to the survival of non-profit businesses as it is to other businesses. To survive and grow, the money coming into the business (revenues) must equal or exceed that going out (expenditure).

1.2 The stereotyping of business sectors

In our exploration of 'what is a business?' another important point is that people often have rather stereotyped perceptions of what different businesses are 'like', particularly if they have never worked in one. The popular image of a business, often reinforced by business study textbooks, is that of a large enterprise, probably in the manufacturing sector, and maybe in the USA: businesses such as Shell, Ford and Johnson & Johnson. This is a misleading and somewhat outdated notion, as service industries, particularly financial services, now usually form the major part of a nation's economic activities. Also, small businesses typically make up about 90 per cent of business activity within any one country. In the UK, for example, out of an estimated 4.3 million business enterprises at the start of 2004, 99.3 per cent were classified as small (0 to 49 employees). Small businesses (SBS) are the subject of study Session 7 of this book.

Stereotypical views of the divisions between different types of businesses are also common. Businesses in the private sector are usually seen as efficient and solely profit-driven, while those in the public sector are generally seen as slow to respond to developments in the external environment and unwilling to change. Charities and voluntary organisations are often seen as amateurish or innovative, depending on your point of view. Large businesses are viewed as *bureaucratic*, small organisations as unreliable, co-operatives as worthy but difficult to manage, and so on.

Another view of different types of businesses, using the axes of size and goals, is shown in Figure 1.1.

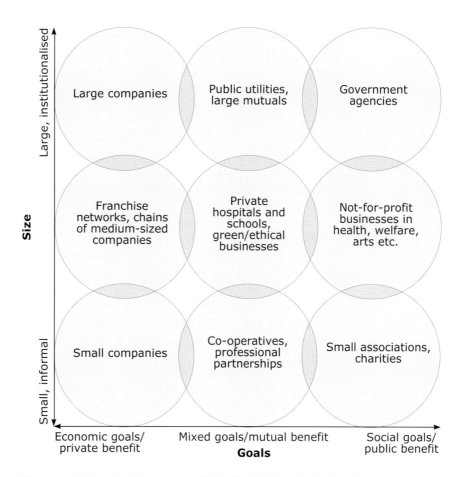

Figure 1.1 Organisations circa 1990, highlighting their diversity

The boundaries between different types of businesses are complex. Large public-sector businesses, such as hospitals and county councils, may well contract out parts of the business to private companies: for example, cleaning, catering and security. *Networking* or collaboration with other similar or different businesses, perhaps in other parts of the world, has become common. The building of the Eurotunnel between France and the UK, for example, was a collaborative project, funded entirely by private investors. In the UK, the government-led Private Finance Initiative (PFI) provides a way for public-sector businesses to raise money for projects in private money markets.

Transferring one way of operating or thinking about business into another business context has been shown to be extremely difficult in a number of cases. Example 1.1 is based on an article written in 2003 by Roy Lilley, a former health authority vice-chair and chair of Homewood NHS Trust from 1990 to 1995. It offers a critical perspective on the problems of introducing private-sector thinking and practices into a public-sector business organisation like the UK National Health Service (NHS).

Example 1.1

So far the extra millions poured into the NHS have produced almost no lasting improvement. More patients through the system, true, but seen by the same staff, working in the same ways, paid slightly better for doing the same job.

The stunningly good businesses that excite the prime minister [Tony Blair] are the product of a fanatical obsession with customer needs, ruthless competition, blindingly good information technology (IT) systems, a passion for quality and excellence and flexible staff ... The NHS has none of this ... Were the NHS a business, it would be out of business.

The reason for this reality gap? Doctors, nurses and health managers are largely home grown. Few of them have worked outside the NHS and fewer of them have any clue how a modern business is run.

[The UK government] has made a good start ... [but will struggle] with hospital consultants who are resisting electronic patient booking. It is consultants' secretaries who manage NHS appointments, often juggling them to fit in with commitments in private practice.

IT systems managing patient records means IT systems that can audit outcomes and clinical performance, holding staff to account. Incontestable electronic appraisal is common in business but rare in the NHS ...

A modern, business-like NHS will challenge vested interests, shake up established practice and turn patients into customers. It will be hard labour for the new NHS and even harder for New Labour [the UK government].

(Source: Lilley, 2003)

In the next activity you will think about your experiences or perceptions of the differences between the public and private business sectors.

Activity 1.2

Spend about **10 minutes** on this activity

Purpose: to reflect on stereotypical and actual differences between the private and public sectors.

Task: first, make a list of how you think people commonly view the private and public sectors. Then, if you have experience of working in the private sector and/or public sector, note down how you think they actually differ. If you have not had work experience, think about your doctor's surgery and your favourite clothes shop. In what ways are they different and why?

Feedback

You may have said that public-sector businesses are viewed as large and slow in decision making, as having infinite resources provided by the State, and as being relatively stress-free places to work, with good pensions and low staff turnover. You may or may not agree with these stereotypical pictures. As we saw in Example 1.1, introducing private-sector thinking – seen as efficient, profit-driven, flexible and responsive – into a large public-sector business such as the NHS is often controversial. This has been a lively area of academic debate. One argument is that, while the language of efficiency is often introduced, the deep-rooted values and objectives of public-sector business will always prevent fundamental change. Others question the desirability of encouraging all businesses to adopt a particular way of thinking and operating. Points of difference from other businesses can be a major factor in an organisation's success.

We have begun to see how business can mean many things, depending not least on the sector in which it operates. The main message of this book is how much variety there is among businesses across the world. As students of business, we need to be aware of both the similarities and the differences between businesses. We also need to be aware that there are many theories and perspectives that can help our analysis and understanding. One famous academic theory, by Gareth Morgan (1986), uses *metaphors* – figures of speech, often used for emphasis or clarity – to illuminate and extend our thinking regarding the question, 'what is a business' Morgan's theory is described in the next section.

1.3 Morgan's metaphors

In *Images of Organization*, Gareth Morgan (1986) talks about learning the skill of 'reading' situations. He suggests this is particularly important for people dealing with business situations: 'skilled readers develop the knack of reading the situations with various scenarios in mind and of forging actions that seem appropriate to the readings thus obtained' (p. 11). The use of metaphor, he explains, 'implies *a way of thinking and a way of seeing* that pervade how we understand our world generally' (p. 12). A metaphor is a non-literal way of describing a thing or an action in terms of something else, something it reminds us of.

'I don't suppose I need to remind anyone that when I use the term "bite the bullet," I mean it metaphorically.'

Morgan's intention is not to categorise different types of businesses, but to offer different ways of looking at them. Looking at a business through a metaphorical 'lens' can help people to understand their experiences with them, either as employees, consumers or citizens. Morgan (1986, pp. 13–16) invites us to share the 'images of organization' offered by the following eight metaphors:

A *machine* – businesses are often designed and operated as if they are machines, with highly visible structures and procedures. They offer continuity and security, but tend to fit people into jobs rather than allow much creativity.

An *organism* – this means seeing the business as behaving in similar ways to our own biological mechanisms. When the environment around us changes, so do our bodies. Successful businesses are often adaptable and open to change. This may mean that its structures and procedures will be less fixed.

A *brain* – seeing a business as a brain means realising it has to be able to respond to change and also be capable of rational thinking and intelligent change. Being open to inquiry and self-criticism often produces the ability to innovate; as Morgan puts it, businesses become 'learning systems' that are able to self-organise.

A *culture* – when we speak of businesses as cultures, we are referring to the fact that they are made up of sets of values, perspectives and principles, held and sustained by the people who work there. This idea is examined in more detail in study Session 4 of this book.

A *political system* – businesses are not only about structures, cultures and hierarchies, they are also about politics. Politics in this context is about the social relations between individuals and groups in a business that involve authority or power. An ***organisational chart*** that plots the lines of communications between people will reveal some of the politics, but not all.

A *psychic prison* – this more abstract metaphor suggests that some businesses may be constrained by themselves. Conventional, or usual, ways of organising work and thinking about the best way to do it can limit change and the adoption of alternative business strategies. Looking at the business in these terms encourages us to dig beneath the surface and try to see some of the restrictions, real or otherwise, that might affect the business and its ability to operate successfully.

As *flux and transformation* – the secret of understanding business from this perspective, suggests Morgan, lies in understanding the constant change shaping our lives. To truly understand a business, we have to appreciate it as an ever-changing thing; it develops, it grows and it regenerates in order to survive.

A *vehicle for domination* – this metaphor introduces us to the idea that businesses can be, or attempt to be, dominant; that is, they can impose, or try to impose, their will on others. This idea is explored in Book 5 of the course. This perspective again encourages us to dig deeper than surface appearances and to appreciate how business can exert influence and power.

You may already find metaphors a useful way of extending your thinking or point of view, or you may not have tried this method before. Morgan's framework is considered to be useful as one way of understanding businesses. It is not meant to suggest fixed types of businesses; indeed, businesses are likely to be a mix of these different metaphors and can change over time, or according to circumstances. These metaphors, or different ways of thinking about 'what is a business?', can help to highlight the complexities of a business and their potential impact on our lives.

Activity 1.3

Spend about **10 minutes** on this activity

Purpose: to demonstrate the difficulty of describing a business.

Task: if you had to explain what a business was to a visitor from outer space, where would you start? Think of one or two businesses that you are familiar with and make a spontaneous list of some key words that come to mind.

Feedback

This was just a simple exercise to make you stop and think for a moment. Even though you may not have actually visited, worked or shopped at a particular business, you, and those around you, will have an image of what it is like. Some examples we came up with are:

- garden centre – colourful, expensive, leisure, flowers;
- car factory – big, noisy, metal, conveyor belts, robots;
- Amazon (online shopping) – e-commerce, remote, overwhelming, automated, impersonal, innovative;
- theme park – leisure, rides, attractions for children, sweets and ice creams;
- corner shop – small, convenient, friendly, expensive.

1.4 Conclusion

The main objective of this first study session was to get you to begin to reflect on the many different types of businesses which exist all around us. A definition which describes all of them is impossible, but there are certain characteristics we can identify as being common to most. In this course we will be introducing different models and theories which can be used to look at business in slightly different ways. Using metaphors is one way of investigating how a business operates. It is a method that highlights the fact that not all aspects of a business will be immediately obvious.

In the next study session we begin to explore the environment in which a business operates using the **STEEP** model to help us.

1.5 Learning outcomes

By the end of this study session on the question, 'what is a business?' you should be able to:

- discuss some of the things that businesses do;
- differentiate between businesses in the private and public and for-profit and non-profit sectors;
- begin to comment on similarities and differences between businesses;
- use the idea of metaphors to think about businesses from different points of view.

You will have developed your learning by:

- using the B120 glossary on the course website to look up the meanings of important terms used in business studies;
- being introduced to the types of activities and examples you will find throughout B120.

Session 2 The external environment

Why are we studying 'the external environment'? The external environment is literally the world in which the business operates. It is a large and ever-changing place which is made up of other organisations, employees, suppliers, customers and other stakeholders. A business cannot operate without being influenced by, and impacting upon, the external environment.

A key success factor for any type of business is an accurate understanding of the external environment in which it operates. An ongoing, long-term analysis of what is happening in all facets of the external environment means that changes which impact on the business can be monitored, anticipated and dealt with appropriately. External environments can be defined and analysed using the STEEP model which is outlined in Section 2.1. STEEP stands for five factors: sociological, technological, economic, environmental and political. You may find variations on STEEP in some business textbooks, for example, STEP (omitting environment), PEST (in a different order), PESTLE (including legal) and STEEPLE (adding ethical). The idea is the same: that there are several, main external influences on a business.

The **aims and objectives** of study Session 2 are to:

- describe the different facets of the external environment surrounding a business;
- introduce the STEEP model as a means of describing and reflecting upon the external environment of the business;
- analyse the different types of stakeholders that have to be considered by a business and understand their contributions and concerns;
- explain how a SWOT analysis may be useful for a business in understanding the strengths, weaknesses, opportunities and threats in the external environment.

2.1 The STEEP model

The STEEP model uses the five headings of sociological, technological, economic, environmental and political factors.

Sociological factors

Sociological factors that are likely to affect businesses include demographic changes in the age and structure of populations, patterns of work, gender roles, patterns of consumption and the ways in which the culture of a population or country changes and develops. In the UK, for example, many households now have the female partner as the breadwinner due to a decline in traditional industries in some regions. There are also many more individuals aged 60 and over these days, many of whom may prefer to continue working.

Technological factors

Every aspect of life has been affected by information and communications technology (ICT) and it has certainly changed the structure and nature of work and our relationship with business. Technological developments influence the scale and rate of change that businesses face. Developments such as the internet place new challenges on the ability of business to meet customer demands. It is difficult to predict where developing technologies will take us next, but it is possible to focus on the process of technological change and its implications for businesses.

- ICT is lowering the barriers of time and place. While this opens up great global opportunities for businesses, it also means that they can no longer expect the protection they have received in the past. The 'global marketplace' has become a reality. Whatever the business sector, there will be increased competition from other businesses that would once have been unable to enter that market.

- ICT creates new industries. These are not just in the areas of hardware, software and telecommunications, but include start-ups, or new businesses, that the new technology makes possible. These include the world of e-commerce, as well as the many 'direct' companies entering traditional areas, such as insurance and banking, by starting and building their operations solely on the basis of electronic information and communications.

- Many individual jobs and internal service functions have been transformed and are now based largely, or solely, on ICT systems. Examples are production planners, credit controllers and, in some instances, sales people. This can have a major impact on the structure of the business and the organisation of work. It has also led to a massive shift in the skills needed for most jobs; some level of computer literacy is now essential for many jobs.

Example 2.1

unionjackwear.co.uk is a one-person business established in 1999 as a hobby by a person with an interest in computers and the internet and an eye for a business opportunity. Starting with five products and a turnover of £500, it is now a full-time job for its owner and stocks over 250 lines, showing a turnover of £77,000 in 2004. The products are advertised and sold through the internet site established and maintained by the owner. The business is now located in a rented storage facility in a local town, and operates a 'just in time' mode of supply, depending on the orders received. Human resource management is not an issue as it is a one-person operation, although the negative aspects of working alone have to be contended with.

An important form of marketing for this business is to have a good web presence on search engines such as Google and MSN and to promote the company through various publications, such as the BBC's *Last Night of the Proms* magazine, VE Day 60th Anniversary official booklets, and also expatriates' websites around the world. Specific Union Jack products are sent to television companies and programmes around the world, creating free marketing opportunities. Social and cultural factors in the external environment were also important in the success of unionjackwear.co.uk. Since the business was established, England has seen a wave of nationalism and an increased demand for items portraying the Union flag. In 2005 there was a call for St George's Day (commemorating the patron saint of England) to be a made a national holiday. Demand for merchandise increased when England won the Rugby World Cup (2003) and participated in the football World Cup (2002) and the Olympic Games (2004). London hosting the Olympics in 2012 should also boost demand.

Economic factors

The economic environment is extremely influential and the activity of world money markets and financial institutions affects businesses in a number of ways. Important factors include the rate of economic growth, *interest rates*, inflation, energy prices, *exchange rates* and levels of employment. The state of a country's economy pervades all aspects of business life. It affects the level of demand for goods and services, the availability and cost of raw materials, buildings and land and, most importantly, labour.

Both businesses and individuals behave according to their expectations of economic trends. If they expect growth to be high, businesses are likely to invest and expand and individuals to spend more. These actions stimulate economic growth and so ensure that the expectations are met. Of course, the same happens in reverse. If the economy is expected to contract, businesses invest less and individuals spend less. Again, the expectation is then fulfilled. Governments use changes in the interest rate to try to achieve short-term adjustment in the levels of demand and investment and spending.

'The trend in tough economic times is to put off everything that doesn't require immediate action – as this chart shows.'

Another important economic variable that can have a major impact on business is the exchange rate. This is the price of a particular *currency*, and is based on the supply and demand for that currency. Global communication technology has resulted in very high levels of *currency trading*, much of it speculative in nature, and this leads to great volatility in exchange rates. Varying exchange rates cause problems for businesses, although many try to minimise risk through forms of insurance. If the domestic currency strengthens (that is, becomes worth more in relation to other currencies), exporting becomes more difficult because the price of goods exported is higher and foreign products are more competitive in the home market. If the currency weakens, exports are easier and opportunities may open up for new markets, while imports become more expensive.

Environmental factors

Environmental issues are of growing importance as people all around the world are much more concerned than ever before about the impact of businesses on the natural environment.

Activity 2.1

Spend about **10 minutes** on this activity

Purpose: to think about how environmental awareness can be used as part of the marketing strategy of a business.

Task: list any 'green' businesses you can think of; that is, businesses that have attempted to cultivate their customer base by establishing and promoting a green image.

Feedback

'Green' can be interpreted in an ecological or ethical way. The number of businesses trying to market themselves as green relates to the demand for organic foods and products that continues to grow despite their higher costs. Many food packets, such as breakfast cereals, heavily promote their 'wholewheat' credentials. Beauty products and toiletries promote their 'natural' ingredients. For example, Herbal Essences shampoos claim a 'special blend of organic herbs and botanicals that come to us in mountain spring water'.

Businesses need to consider a number of environmental factors.

- *Legislation*: in many countries, environmental legislation is increasing. The main emphasis is on pollution control and waste disposal, but regulation is also affecting packaging, transport and distribution, and sources of materials.
- *Information*: in recognition of the interests of the local community and the broader public, many businesses now report regularly on their environmental performance. Larger businesses may carry out regular environmental audits and publish them in their annual reports.
- *Employees*: increasingly, employees are interested in and concerned about the environmental credentials of their employers. Businesses may wish to

maintain good communications with their employees, listening to their opinions and reporting back on a regular basis.

- *Shareholders:* most **shareholders** of larger businesses are financial institutions whose interests are driven by financial performance. In several countries, however, a category of ethical, or 'green', investors is emerging, and businesses may wish to consider whether they should present themselves as eligible for such investments (study Session 5 of this book looks at **business ethics**).

- *Pressure groups*: there was a massive growth in pressure groups in the late twentieth century. Although many of them were established to tackle single issues, they frequently broadened their membership bases and became a permanent part of the political scene. One example is how consumer groups have fought to get the levels of salt and fat in foods lowered. Stonewall and Greenpeace are examples of pressure groups who have grown significantly in terms of members. The challenge to business from lobbyists and consumers is explained in Book 5 of this course.

- *Customers:* there are opportunities for businesses operating to high environmental standards to gain market advantage. Some customers are willing to favour 'green' organisations, which may increase the market share of the business or enable higher prices to be charged for their goods or services.

Political factors

Political influences control or affect most of what we all do. There are political influences on business in terms of rules and regulations imposed by government (local, national or global), as well as the influences of such organisations as chambers of commerce, trade unions and co-operatives.

The following list can only hint at the importance of political factors for business.

- Legislation affects many aspects of business life, such as health and safety at work, equal opportunities and employee protection. The Chartered Institute of Personnel and Development's website (enter CIPD into an internet search engine) contains information on the ever-changing area of employment law.

- Trading relationships are strongly influenced by political factors. The **World Trade Organization** and the **European Union** are examples of this.

- Government is a major party to many transactions. In all countries, the government is one of the largest employers and the largest purchaser of goods and services. In some cases, such as defence, medicines and some social services, the government is virtually the only customer.

- The level and nature of public services – for example, health services, education and the police force – are determined on political grounds.

- Governments determine levels of taxation – on the individual, on businesses, on property and on goods and services.

The following example is an extract from a *Financial Times* article written in 2003 by Paul Taylor about US airlines. You will need to read this example to complete Activity 2.2 which follows. Look at the task for this activity before reading Example 2.2.

Example 2.2

Political attack

US business travellers have been forced to put up with upheaval in airport security systems in the wake of the September 11 [2001] terrorist attacks, the bankruptcy filings of two big airlines, and drastic changes in fares and frequent flyer programmes.

Economical

Many are now complaining that airlines, fighting for survival in the midst of one of the industry's worst-ever downturns, are [harassing] them with measures designed to squeeze additional revenues out of passengers or cut back on perks and benefits.

For example, many airlines have tightened up existing cabin baggage regulations and have begun to strictly enforce excess baggage charges – moves designed to garner additional revenues but which run the risk of alienating many business and other passengers.

Several recent newspaper articles have featured passengers who have been charged hundreds of dollars for an extra bag. Business travellers in particular complain that the premium prices they pay for their tickets are not reflected in standards of service.

Technological

Other airlines have begun to charge an additional fee of up to $25 if passengers insist on using paper tickets instead of electronic ones. Until they reversed themselves a few weeks ago, many of the big airlines had also begun to charge passengers $100 if they wanted to fly standby on flights on the same day as their originally scheduled flights...

Economical

US passengers also face the prospect of fewer scheduled flights ... industry executives and analysts believe United [Airlines] will have to cut back its route system substantially and negotiate further substantial concessions from its employees if it is to survive.

They warn that if United manages to restructure ... it will be a very different airline to the globe-straddling carrier that profited handsomely, selling high-price last-minute tickets to business travellers during the economic boom of the late 1990s.

Political + Economical

A more immediate concern is that the increasingly likely prospect of a war with Iraq could cause oil prices to spike, further undermining the shaky health of many US airlines and leading to the possibility that other carriers could go bust.

Economical

But even without an oil price spike, the traditional carriers in the US were already facing fierce competition from cut-price operators such as Southwest Airlines and three-year-old upstart, Jet Blue. Most have acknowledged that they will have to slash costs if they are to survive.

Overall, the US airline industry is in a parlous financial state. Last year alone, operators lost about $8bn on top of the more than $7bn they lost in 2001. The six biggest carriers – American, United, Delta Air

Lines, Northwest Airlines, Continental and US Airways – have all suffered badly.

Southwest Airlines was the only significant carrier that did not cut back operations last year and its profitability, amid a sea of losses, has earned it a stock market value bigger than all its rivals combined.

Governmental

This is not the first time the US airline industry has been plunged into financial turmoil. Since the government deregulated the industry in 1978, it has faced two serious recessions in the early 1980s and 1990s.

Economical

But the combination of the fear created by the September 2001 terrorist attacks, competition from cut price airlines and the growing sophistication of travellers who now have access to comparative fare information via the internet makes this downturn different, say analysts.

Economical

The success of low cost 'no-frills' carriers in lucrative markets such as California and the east coast has destroyed the traditional carriers' profits on many routes that they once dominated. For example, Southwest Airlines' share of the California market has jumped to more than 60 per cent in the 18 months, while United's share has fallen to less than 20 per cent, in part because losses have forced the big carrier to cut back on its flights

Faced with the success of the low price carriers and the underlying downturn in passenger traffic, most carriers have been forced to cut their already heavily discounted economy fares further. According to estimates, the average price to fly a mile, adjusted for inflation, fell by 25 per cent in the 10 years to 2001.

Since they were unable to raise the prices they charged leisure travellers for fares booked well in advance, most big carriers have raised prices for last minute bookings and business fares. In some cases a business ticket is now almost six times as expensive as a discount ticket.

The widening gap between business and discounted economy fares has prompted many companies to re-examine their business travel policies, cancel trips and in some cases abandon the deals they had previously negotiated with big carriers.

At the same time, the internet has made it much easier for both business and leisure travellers to compare prices and tinker with itineraries in order to save money.

With the continuing uncertainty over the US economic recovery and geopolitics, the big carriers are unlikely to find much relief this year. For business travellers, that may translate into further uncertainty and turmoil.

(Source: Taylor quoted in Capon, 2004, pp. 276–7)

Activity 2.2

Spend about **1 hour** on this activity

Purpose: to look at the effects of STEEP factors on a real business.

Task: read Example 2.2. Note down and reflect on the different influences that have affected US airlines, using the STEEP headings of sociological, technological, economic, environmental and political factors in your note taking.

Feedback

You will have noted how the political context in which the airline industry in the USA is situated had a direct impact on the US airlines' business. After the terrorist attacks in New York in September 2001, passengers were afraid to fly and the social and cultural attitudes of a nation used to using airlines as a very common form of transport were shaken. Two economic factors affecting airlines worldwide were increasing oil prices and the introduction of low cost airlines. No one could have predicted the success of low cost airlines, which was greatly influenced by technological developments that allow searching for, shopping and booking tickets online. Attempts to cut operating costs led to fewer flights and unpredictable supply, which affected consumers' perception of the business and industry. The main environmental issue in this case would be the pollutant effects on the environment caused by the increased number of flights available through the low cost airlines. This may further reduce overall demand for air travel. None of this could have been predicted, even perhaps with the existence of a reliable external environment monitoring system such as STEEP.

The STEEP model provides a useful structure for the discussion of the external environment. As you will have noted, however, the distinction between the factors is rather artificial. Many political decisions have an economic impact, and almost all economic factors have a political dimension. Social behaviour is influenced by new technology, and in turn influences political decisions. Environmental issues have strong social, political and economic elements, and the introduction of environmentally acceptable solutions often depends on the adoption of new technology.

In the next section we begin to explore the impact on a business of its stakeholders, those 'individuals, groups and other organizations that have interests (their stake) in the activities and outcomes of the organization' (Hatch, 1997, p. 121).

2.2 Stakeholders

Stakeholders are people, or groups, who have a legitimate interest in the activities of businesses and other organisations in their society. Employees, customers and shareholders are all examples of stakeholders. Others include managers, suppliers, local communities and the State (in the form of institutions, citizens and taxpayers). In the voluntary sector, for example, stakeholders include funders, sponsors and donors. In the public sector they include the general public in their capacity as citizens (through elected representatives), as taxpayers (funders) and as beneficiaries of public services (customers).

A stakeholder framework for a for-profit business (see section 1.1 in study Session 1) is shown in Table 2.1.

Table 2.1 Stakeholders and their expectations

Stakeholders		Expectations
	Primary	**Secondary**
Owners	Financial return	**Capital growth**
Employees	Pay	Work satisfaction, training, social integration
Customers	Supply of goods/ services	**Quality**
Creditors	**Creditworthiness**	Security
Suppliers	Payment	Long-term relationships
Community	Safety and security	Contribution to the community
Government	Compliance	Improved competitiveness

The concept of stakeholders is important for two reasons. First, it emphasises that stakeholder groups have different interests; second, it illustrates the relationship between businesses and their external environments (as explained through the STEEP model in the previous section).

There are four important points that you should bear in mind with regard to the stakeholders of a business.

1   All businesses have internal stakeholders: shareholders, employees, managers, directors, trustees. They also have stakeholders external to the business but strongly linked to or affected by it. These include customers/ clients, suppliers, funders and, possibly, competitors. There are also external stakeholders who are indirectly affected by the business, who might include members of the community or the general public.

2   Different stakeholders have different interests, and these interests may be in conflict. We can easily recognise the conflict between the interests of employees, who want security of employment and increased earnings, and those of shareholders, who may be seeking short-term cost reductions. A similar conflict could exist between the interests of taxpayers and of those who receive public services such as education or health.

3   The culture, structure and control systems within a business will determine how these conflicts, or trade-offs, are resolved, and in practice the interests of one stakeholder group often have a dominant position. Commercial businesses are conventionally considered to be shareholder-led, although the reality is that directors and senior managers may have the dominant interests. Some service industries may be regarded as customer-led. Some public and voluntary services can be considered staff-led. Co-operatives tend to be member-led.

4   Some stakeholder interests are protected by law, but not all. Owners and shareholders are protected by property and company law, whereas the

interests of other stakeholders are protected, if at all, only by regulation or management discretion. In many countries, measures have been taken in recent years to adjust this imbalance: employment legislation provides increasing protection for employees; and environmental legislation and regulation limit shareholders' profits, to the benefit of local communities and the environment in general.

Activity 2.3

Spend about **15 minutes** on this activity

Purpose: to reinforce understanding of the different interests and levels of power of stakeholders.

Task: consider the four statements below and attempt the following two questions:

What do the statements say about conflicting stakeholder interests?

Which is the dominant stakeholder group in each case?

1 'The health service has always been customer-focused; but it has always defined its customers as the doctors.' (*A senior nurse.*)

2 'These people – they think they own the place.' (*A head teacher to a colleague following a conversation with a parent.*)

3 'You can have any colour you like, as long as it's black.' (*Henry Ford, the car manufacturer.*)

4 'Our people are our greatest asset – and the fewer of them the better.' (*From a company's annual report.*)

Feedback

1 There is clearly a conflict here between the interests of doctors, other clinical staff and patients. The implication is that the dominant stakeholders are the doctors. No mention is made of the interests of the taxpayers, who are funding the health service.

2 Who does 'own the place'? The professionals (teachers here) may see the school as theirs. But so may parents, students, the local community and taxpayers – all 'customers' with a claim to ownership.

3 This is the classic statement of industrial arrogance: the presumption of the dominant interests of shareholders and directors over those of customers.

4 In this example, lip service is paid to one stakeholder group, the employees, but the real dominance lies with shareholders and directors.

All types of businesses have difficulty balancing the interests of their different stakeholders, particularly when the political reality is that different groups have different amounts of power. For example:

- Commercial businesses have structures that recognise the dominance of shareholders: shareholders appoint directors, who appoint managers, who manage the interests of other stakeholders. However, the legislative and regulatory environment, over, for example CO_2 emissions, is increasingly imposing constraints to protect the interests of other stakeholder groups.

- Voluntary organisations are usually less rigidly structured, and priorities may depend on the power of their management committees or trustees. Employees may exhibit greater dominance than those in the commercial sector.

- Government bodies are accountable to taxpayers and to service users, both represented by elected representatives (politicians); in some instances, the reality is that the dominant stakeholder is the employee.

In the next activity, which is based on an essential reading at the back of this book, you will continue your learning about stakeholders. We have included this essential reading because understanding stakeholders is a key part of understanding business.

Activity 2.4

Spend about **2 hours** on this activity

Purpose: to learn more about the stakeholders of a business.

Task: read Essential Reading 1, 'Analysing stakeholders' by Claire Capon, which is at the back of this book. This extract uses a diagram to explain different types of stakeholder, then uses the example of the Automobile Association (AA) to illustrate this learning.

Make notes as you go along and keep them for further reference and revision. If there is anything you are unclear about, make a note to ask your tutor about it. Alternatively you could post it as a topic of discussion for your online tutor group forum. If you need help with note taking, contacting tutors, or the tutor group forum, please consult your B120 Study Companion.

Feedback

This is the first of a type of activity used in B120 which is based on an essential reading. These readings are reproduced at the back of the book and are included in your total study hours. Essential readings are also noted in the B120 Study Companion, where you will find extra questions and reflective activities to ensure that you have got the most from them.

Conflict between stakeholders

To end this section on stakeholders, it is important to note that there is always potential for conflict between the interests of any and all stakeholders in a business. Possible conflicts include those between the following.

- *Shareholders and customers* Customers want high quality and low prices, while shareholders are interested in minimising costs and maximising profits. In reality, however, these differences will be primarily about timescales. In the long term, shareholders and customers are interdependent and therefore have a shared interest in value for money.

- *Managers and shareholders* Attitudes towards salaries, perks and business risk are likely to be different, but ultimately the interests of shareholders are dominant. They employ directors and managers as agents to run the business on their behalf.

- *Funding agencies and service users*   In public or voluntary services, there is typically a greater demand for services than the available funds can support, and choices have to be made to ration the services provided or compromise on their quality.

It is easy to take a simplified view of the relationship between business and society. On the one hand, some people argue that the aim of business is to do good in the world. On the other hand, some economists claim that the business of business is simply to make profits and that it is not for business managers to make judgements about the needs of society, that that is the concern of others, such as politicians. Like most simplified views, these are probably both wrong, or at least overstated. The reality is that society and business depend on each other – businesses are part of society and vice versa – and, like all forms of interdependence, this provides benefits, but also imposes obligations on both parties. This is discussed further in the next section.

2.3 Business and society

The role of business is primarily economic. Unless a business performs its economic functions it will not have the resources to perform other roles, nor will it survive long enough to be an agent for any form of change. Businesses exist to produce goods and provide services that society wants and needs, at a profit, and they cannot take on additional responsibilities unless they perform these tasks successfully. At the same time, business depends for its survival and long-term prosperity on society providing the resources – people, raw materials, services and infrastructure – which it needs to operate profitably.

Society also provides other, less tangible, inputs to business. These include:

- a means of exchange (money);
- a legal system that is effectively policed and enforced;
- defence and trade arrangements.

All these, in turn, depend on the members of the society supporting the values and norms that the business endorses. There is therefore an implied contract between businesses and the communities in which they operate. A business is expected to create wealth, supply markets, generate employment, innovate and contribute to the maintenance of the community in which it is situated. Businesses, including their shareholders and other stakeholders, depend on the communities in which they operate for their existence and prosperity. The fundamental role of business is to provide the means by which the needs of the community are met, in the form of goods and services, jobs and income from taxes paid by the companies and their employees. The infrastructure on which industry depends requires long-term commitments (hospitals, schools and so on), and communities expect that businesses will match this with long-term investments. Business is also required to act legally and responsibly with respect to health and safety at work, employment conditions and environmental issues.

So, how do businesses in practice reconcile the demand for greater profit, lower costs, or 'more for less', with the interests of society to secure employment, protection of the environment and tax income? There is not a simple answer to this question, but the following points may be of help.

- The degree of conflict between maximising profit and serving the interests of the community will depend on the type of business and its relationship with the community. If it is a major employer in the area, or a major customer of local suppliers, then its actions are going to have a substantial impact on the community. The community is a major stakeholder, and there are correspondingly serious obligations on the business to consider the interests and views of the local community when making decisions. This is likely to be in its interests because it will probably depend on local support for business plans. However, increasing globalisation can weaken a business's ties with its local community. Its headquarters may be in one country, its plant managers from another, its suppliers from yet another, and its profits accounted for in whichever country it is most tax efficient to do so.

- It is important that there is communication between the business and its stakeholders. This can be at both the formal and the informal level. Many businesses, for example, encourage their employees to participate in local activities. Typically, companies are good at communicating when they want something, such as planning permission, but allow communication links to lapse when there are no pressing needs.

- Many decisions that may seem quite trivial to a business may be of great importance to the local community. An example would be the routeing of delivery trucks. Unnecessary bad feeling can be avoided if the community's interests are taken into account.

- Environmental issues often create tension. Businesses may seek to operate to the lowest legally permissible standards, and may thereby create distrust and suspicion among local residents. On the other hand, local opposition may be voiced through pressure groups that are overtly anti-industry and whose arguments are therefore instinctively rejected by companies, even when they express valid concerns.

The relationship between business and society is covered in a relatively new area of business literature under the title *corporate social responsibility (CSR)*. Business ethics is introduced in study Session 5 of this book, and CSR is discussed in more detail in Book 5, where 'alternative' views of business are introduced.

Many businesses have CSR policies, and these are sometimes clearly stated on the business website. The retail giant Tesco, for example, dedicates several pages to CSR policies on its corporate website.

2.4 SWOT analysis

SWOT stands for strengths, weaknesses, opportunities and threats. An analysis of these gives the business an overview of its position in relation to its external environment. The strengths and weaknesses of a business arise from its internal environment; that is, resources and their use, structure (outlined in study Session 3 of this book), culture (study Session 4) and the different business functions (study Session 6). Which strengths a business decides to build upon and which it seeks to minimise depends on the impact of opportunities and threats from the external environment. Once the external influences on a business have been identified, they can then be judged to be either a threat or an opportunity and can be dealt with, or taken advantage of, as appropriate.

The next activity, based on another essential reading from Capon (2004), provides a more detailed explanation of SWOT and SWOT analysis.

Activity 2.5

Spend about **2 hours** on this activity

Purpose: to find out more about SWOT and to apply your learning to a real business situation.

Task: read Essential Reading 2, 'Strengths, weaknesses, opportunities and threats' by Claire Capon, which is at the back of this book.

Make notes as you go along and keep them for further reference and revision. If there is anything you are unclear about, make a note to ask your tutor about it or post it as a topic of discussion for your tutor group forum.

Feedback

Don't be tempted to skip this activity. Your notes on Essential Reading 2 will help you in your understanding of the SWOT concept. SWOT analysis is used in all types of business and business functions.

SWOT analysis relating to business functions

One method of undertaking a SWOT analysis is to consider strengths, weaknesses opportunities and threats in relation to four key business functions: marketing, operations, human resources and finance. This type of SWOT analysis is shown in Table 2.2, which is an example from Capon (2004) based on an analysis of the MPW restaurant, owned by the chef Marco Pierre White and his joint-venture partner Granada.

Table 2.2 SWOT analysis for the MPW restaurant using strengths, weaknesses, opportunities and threats and four functions

	Marketing	Operations	Human resources	Finance
Strengths	• Marco Pierre White and MPW name. • Imaginative menu.	• Some dishes served in the restaurant are greatly enjoyed by the diners.	• Good chef, responsible for cooking and maybe putting together imaginative menu.	• Joint venture with Granada will be an asset, particularly if a chain of MPW restaurants is developed throughout the UK, as Granada has experience in managing chains of catering outlets. • Dishes on the menu are reasonably priced.
Weaknesses	None mentioned in the case study.	• Poor service from both waiting staff and the receptionist • Some dishes served in the restaurant are not enjoyed by the diners.	• Staff overworked during busy periods and offering poor service outside peak periods.	None mentioned in the case study.
Opportunities	• Expansion around the UK, aim to have a MPW in every major city.	None mentioned in the case study.	None mentioned in the case study.	None mentioned in the case study.
Threats	• Other restaurants, particularly those that have a celebrity chef, like Anthony Worrall Thompson or Gary Rhodes.	• The possibly reducing number of locations available to expand into, particularly in London. This will be affected by the increasing number of similar restaurant chains seeking to expand in the same way and possibly drive up the cost of suitable locations that do exist.	• Other restaurants opening in London and seeking to expand may seek to poach staff, particularly a talented chef who is a good cook and able to put together an imaginative menu.	• If MPW is not very successful, Granada may choose to withdraw from the joint venture and cease to provide any expected financial resources.

(Source: Capon, 2004, pp. 401–2)

It can be seen from Table 2.2 that the main *threats* arise from other restaurants, particularly if they develop chains and move into locations in which MPW may be interested. MPW is, therefore, going to have to act quickly to obtain desirable locations. MPW is also going to have to seek to retain good staff and prevent them from being poached by other expanding chains. It is going to have to ensure a good and stable relationship with its joint-venture partner, the Granada group.

Capon suggests that the key *opportunity* for MPW is expansion beyond London, via a strategy of market penetration and development that involves offering the same type of reasonably priced food in cities around the UK.

The principal *weaknesses* arise from staff working at top speed during peak periods and not being able to offer a high quality of service in the quieter times that directly follow those peak periods. This is likely to influence some customers' opinions of the business.

The fundamental *strengths* of MPW undoubtedly rest with both its name and the imaginative and high-quality food offered at reasonable prices. These strengths are key factors for success in the restaurant business. Therefore these strengths, supported by a sound joint venture with Granada, put MPW in a convincing position to pursue an expansion, or 'rollout', of MPW restaurants.

This business example should have helped your understanding of what a SWOT analysis is and how it can be used to assess and plan for business developments.

2.5 Conclusion

This study session discussed the complicated world in which business operates and introduced various methods that businesses use to analyse the external world. The STEEP model is a useful reminder that we should consider all influences on a business: the sociological, technological, economic, environmental and political. Understanding the different stakeholders of a business, including the wider society in which it operates, is another important aspect of the external environment. We introduced the notion of corporate social responsibility (CSR), a relatively new business concept which will be discussed in more detail in Books 4 and 5. In short, CSR refers to the relationship between a business and its stakeholders from an ethical perspective. A SWOT analysis can provide a useful overview of a business's position in relation to its external environment. It is important that businesses can use such models, concepts and tools to help them make sense of the volatile world in which they operate and within which business decisions have to be made.

In the next study session we look at how the choice of structure in a business affects the way in which the business operates.

2.6 Learning outcomes

By the end of this study session on the external environment of the business you should be able to:

- describe the STEEP model used to understand the influences in the external environment impacting on business;
- understand the different social, technological, economic, environmental and political factors affecting business;
- explain the difference between internal and external stakeholders in a business and their sources of power and influence;
- understand the relationship between business and the society in which it is situated;

- offer a simple definition of corporate social responsibility;
- perform a simple SWOT analysis on a specific business situation.

You will have developed your learning by:

- reading and taking notes on Essential Readings 1 and 2;
- seeing how theoretical models such as SWOT are used in real life business organisations (in this case the MPW restaurant);
- exploring more about specific business cases by studying examples.

Session 3 Business structures

Why are we studying 'business structures'? A structure gives a business an identity and provides continuity. It also provides a framework for the allocation of roles and responsibilities. All businesses will have some sort of structure, depending on the product or service they provide, but also influenced by the history, size and culture of that business.

Most businesses have some sort of organisational chart, and that chart will provide clues about the structure of the business. The chart will show the formal relationships between different individuals and departments, and provide an outline of the official decision-making structure. Those positions higher in the chart usually have more power and authority than those lower down. The shape of the organisational chart can tell us much about the way in which the business works, and perhaps the values behind this. For example, some organisational charts are narrow and tall, with many levels of authority, while a wider, flatter chart might suggest a business where there are fewer levels of authority and the distance between higher and lower level positions is perhaps less important to how the business operates. Structure also includes the arrangements by which various activities are divided between the members of the business and the ways in which their efforts are co-ordinated.

The **aims and objectives** of study Session 3 are to:

- communicate the advantages and disadvantages of structuring a business;
- explain the differences between formal and informal business structures;
- familiarise you with some of the main types of business structure;
- consider some of the variables that can be explored to identify structures within business.

3.1 Different types of structure

Issues about structure are recurring matters of debate and dispute in most businesses. This is because they include matters relating to departmental and sectional groups, the pattern of reporting relationships, the cycle of meetings, information systems, and rules and procedures.

A business might be structured in various ways: by function, by product, by service or by geography. These four types are shown in Figure 3.1.

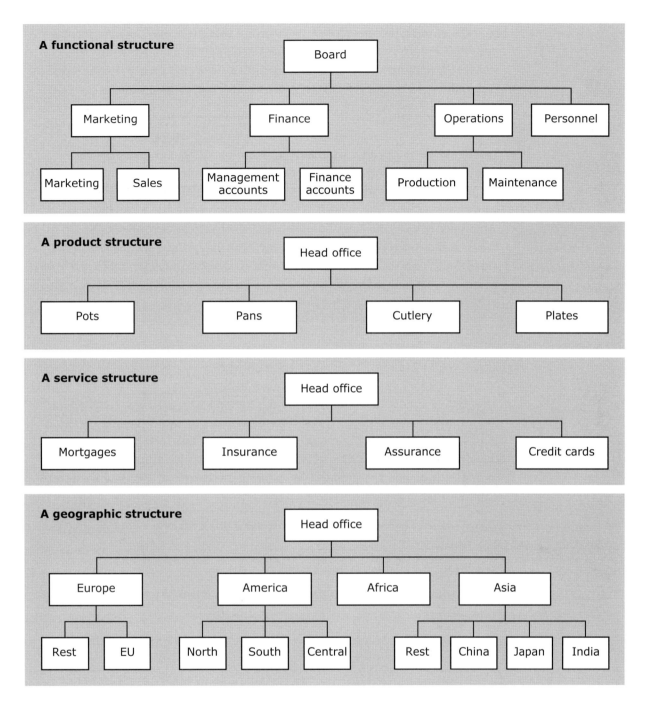

Figure 3.1 Examples of functional, product, service and geographical organisational structures

As is the case with most aspects of business, it is unlikely that there is any one 'best' model for structure. You would not expect businesses with a professional orientation, such as a legal or medical practice, or a not-for-profit business such as a church or theatre company with a strong values base, to have the same business or management structure as a supermarket or high street bank. The structure of a co-operative would enable the broad-based participation and involvement of its members, while a legal practice would need a more collectivist or collegiate structure. The challenge facing all types of businesses is to develop a structure that recognises what is required while still achieving an efficient use of resources and providing effective services to customers.

Whatever the business, however, structure is pivotal in the relationship between *task* (what the business does) and *process* (how the business does it). It is through the medium of its structure that the values, commitments, purposes and aspirations of the business are implemented. Structure has to translate values and processes into a practical, working reality – and to do this while delivering profit to its owners and value to its customers.

Functional structures might work best when departments need regular communication with each other. However, a disadvantage may be that functions and the people who work in them may become rather insular. Structuring by product or service can help to achieve better responsiveness to customer needs, although it might mean professional or functional expertise becomes fragmented. A geographic structure has advantages for a large international business because there are likely to be differences between the markets it serves. There are also likely to be language and cultural differences. However, structuring by location may be problematic in terms of communication and information flows, and support functions such as finance and ICT may have to be duplicated.

3.2 Why have a structure?

Structure is concerned with the most appropriate way to group activities in the business to be able to achieve desired objectives. Considerable variation is possible in terms of the types of structure. Structure will be influenced by the size of the business, the technology it employs, the behaviour of groups within it, management strategy, the external environment and the history and culture of the business.

Activity 3.1

Spend about **10 minutes** on this activity

Purpose: to consider the problems of trying to run a business without a structure.

Task: make a list of some possible problems of trying to run a structureless business.

Feedback

You may have considered the following points.

- It would not be clear who was and who was not part of the business.
- There would be no way of getting objectives agreed and hence of measuring success.
- There would be no agreed way of making decisions.
- All decisions could be open to reconsideration whenever anyone was unhappy with them.
- It would not be clear who should do what work.
- Individuals and other bodies in the external environment would not know whom to contact.

Jo Freeman gives an even stronger rationale for the need for formal structure:

> Contrary to what we would like to believe, there is no such thing as a 'structureless' group. Any group of people of whatever nature, coming together for any length of time, for any purpose, will inevitably structure itself in some fashion. The structure may be flexible, it may vary over time, and it may evenly or unevenly distribute tasks, power and resources over the members of the group. But it will be formed regardless of the abilities, personalities or intentions of the people involved ...
>
> For everyone to have the opportunity to be involved in a given group and to participate in its activities the structure must be explicit, not implicit. The rules of decision making must be open and available to everyone, and this can happen only if they are formalised. This is not to say that formalisation of a group structure will destroy the informal structure. It usually doesn't. But it does hinder the informal structure from having predominant control and makes available some means of attacking it. 'Structurelessness' is organisationally impossible. We cannot decide whether to have a structured or a structureless group; only whether or not to have a formally structured one.
>
> (Freeman, 1972–3, pp. 152–3)

By pulling these arguments together, we can identify four advantages for a business of having a clear and public structure.

1   Enabling participation. The structure of any business will determine how all the relevant sections and parties join in its activities and influence its decisions. In other words, the structure underpins how power and accountability, internal and external, operate within the business. Indeed, the more complex the stakeholder pattern, and the more contested the control over the business's purposes, the more complex the structures. It is no accident that a business such as Unilever, the European Union, or a university have highly complex structures and procedures. The rules generally enable people to find their way around, co-ordinate activity, make decisions and participate. Without them, there might be anarchy and chaos. Lessons may be drawn here from the plight of some former communist states in Eastern Europe when the strong structures of the previous regimes collapsed.

2   Providing a framework for the allocation of responsibilities and authority. Structure is at the heart of the differentiation and integration of work. More simply, it is structure that makes it clear who is doing what and helps people to work together. The more appropriate the structure, the more effective the working relationships between individuals and departments. Defining the responsibilities of sections, their staff and their managers, and establishing patterns of communication and information flows between them, are aspects of structure that are likely to impinge most immediately and obviously on people's work.

3   Establishing an identity for the business. Any business will need to allocate responsibilities for external contacts. For example, suppliers and

customers need to be able to identify whom to contact within the business. Legal documents have to be signed and procedures established for the recruitment of staff. More broadly, the structure of the business and the way people work within it convey messages to the outside world about the values and character of that business.

4 Continuity and change. Many businesses deal with change and uncertainty. Structure can provide continuity. Without a structure, there is a tendency for people to constantly set up new systems and procedures – to reinvent the wheel – in response to new situations.

There are, of course, disadvantages to well-established structures. They can, for example, be difficult to change. This underlines the importance of seeing structure as dynamic, and not static. As in most aspects of business, there is no such thing as a 'one size fits all' model.

The challenge is to develop a structure for the business that meets the requirements and still achieves an efficient use of resources and the provision of effective services to customers.

People who establish new businesses or projects often pay scant attention to structure. The strong motivation people feel when they are involved in a new project can mean that the business functions more by goodwill than by well thought-out structures and procedures. As the business grows, however, problems that stem from this lack of attention to structure will become apparent.

It should by now be apparent why the structure of a business is fundamental, not only to its effective functioning and the achievement of its objectives, but also to its meaning and identity.

3.3 Formal and informal structures

The organisational chart of a business, discussed earlier, provides a pictorial and formal – that is, agreed and written down – explanation of the different parts of the business and the different jobs within it. A chart will show the distribution of, and relationship between, the roles in the business rather than say anything about the individuals who fill them. The other side of the structure of any business is the informal one, which is less likely to be written down on the organisational chart. The informal structure is more about the relationships between individuals. This can be complicated because it involves the 'human' elements such as respect, compatibility, motivation and commitment; in other words, it is about the 'chemistry' that exists between people that always affects both relationships and results.

'Yes, you are speaking to grandma'

This next activity will help you to explore the distinction between formal and informal structures.

Activity 3.2

Spend about **30 minutes** on this activity

Purpose: to consider formal and informal structures by reflecting on your experience of differences with someone 'in charge' of you.

Task: think of a situation from your life or work experience where you were working with a person who was officially in charge of you and/or the group. You were formally expected to do what they asked you to do, however, they appeared to have different values to yourself and you did not feel they were the right person for the job. Think very carefully about the situation and the person and make notes about the context and the personalities involved. Reflect on the following questions.

1   What was it about the individual's attitudes and behaviour that made you feel that they were the wrong person for the job?

2   What happened in terms of your relationship? Did their behaviour change over time?

3   Did you begin to see some of the reasons behind their decisions and instructions?

4 How did you and/or the group cope with this situation?

Feedback

A chart may tell us about 'official' levels of authority, but we have probably all experienced or witnessed an occasion where a boss was unable to exert their authority, and was not actually in charge. This could be for all sorts of reasons: a particular management style, lack of confidence, etc. They may have been recruited to the wrong job, or promoted above their capabilities, or it could be that they were simply not respected or liked. The BBC's comedy programme *The Office*, for example, has a manager, David Brent, who thinks his style of running his department, having fun, is the way to get the best performance and highest level of liking from his team. He is, in fact, considered to be a bit of a joke. (Enter the search term 'The Office' on the BBC website for more information about this series.)

3.4 Dimensions of structure

Some famous research studies developed at Aston University during the 1970s attempted to identify the main dimensions of business structure (Pugh and Hickson, 1968). Pugh and Hickson examined the following factors, or structural variables, that may be helpful in identifying the type of structure within a business, and the reasons for it:

- *Specialisation* The extent to which specialised tasks and roles are allocated to individuals who work in the business.
- *Standardisation* The extent to which a business has standard procedures.
- *Formalisation* The extent to which rules, procedures, instructions and so on are written down, or formalised.
- *Centralisation* The extent to which decision making and authority are located at the top of the hierarchical structure and/or at the centre of the business if, for example, there is more than one site.
- *Configuration* The shape of the role structure, whether the chain of command is short or long.

Researchers can use these variables to investigate how and why a business is structured as it is. This is useful for our understanding, but, as stated earlier, explicit, written down clues, such as those in organisational charts, do not always tell us how individuals within the business behave in practice. The arena of the 'unwritten rule' is referred to in business studies as 'organisational culture' (see study Session 4 of this book).

Example 3.1 on the next page, a case study of a non-traditional business, the Football Association in England, demonstrates that the entire performance of a business can be affected by getting the structure of a business wrong.

Returning to the list at the beginning of this section (3.4) based on the research at Aston University on dimensions of business structure, we can now go on to consider some more questions about these different aspects and how they might be implemented practically. First, in terms of specialisation, or the way in which specialised jobs are allocated to groups or individuals in the business, we could ask: *'how much specialisation within the business structure is desirable?'*

Businesses need to devise ways of sharing out the work so that it can be done as effectively as possible. Traditionally, there have been two ways in which jobs have been allocated: first, on the basis of job specialisation, making use of individual expertise, distinctive knowledge, training, skills and competences; and second, by breaking down complex tasks and processes into simpler, routine elements and requiring each worker to concentrate on one or more of these. Conventionally, allocation through job specialisation has been associated with professional, expert work and relies on the skills and judgement of individual workers. In contrast, task breakdown is widely used for production and clerical operations; it provides little opportunity to develop the skills and judgement of individual workers. Specialists can be difficult to manage and their perspectives on the business may be narrow, making it difficult to integrate their contributions with the overall processes of the business. For example, accountants and nurses may see themselves as representatives of their profession and only secondarily as members of the business that employs them. Thus, they may have different loyalties and priorities.

Example 3.1

The [England] Football Association [FA] board and council need radical reform if the modern game is to be effectively governed, according to Lord Burns, who yesterday published the initial findings of his strategic review of the FA. He has concluded that the current structure, in which responsibilities are shared by the board and council, is inadequate ...

In a hard-nosed assessment of tensions between the amateur and professional interests within the FA, Burns says the increasingly commercial, international nature of the modern game has highlighted the FA's organisational flaws.

'These tensions show up the inadequacies of the organisational structures that were not designed with the modern demands of a sporting governing body in mind,' he said. 'The lack of clarity of responsibility, the difficulty in reaching decisions and the substantial frustration and tension that exists undermines the authority and effectiveness of the organisation' ...

The current structure, in which the council retains final decision-making powers, has led to a 'lack of clarity', Burns states ...

The council should be reformed to give a voice to supporters, players, referees, managers, coaches, women, ethnic minorities and disabled groups. He also calls for the amateur and grassroots game to be given a new structure, called the Community Football Alliance, for a clear division of FA income to be instituted, and for the relationships between the FA and the professional leagues to be formalised.

(Source: Kelso, 2005)

Another question we could ask in relation to structuring jobs is: *'how can the business achieve co-ordination?'* Co-ordination is about how the business can align the activities and objectives of the different departments and project teams. As businesses decentralise their activities to improve responsiveness and flexibility in an increasingly volatile and competitive environment, so co-ordination becomes correspondingly more important. For example, few businesses would want each project team or business area to establish its own policy on health and safety or equal opportunities. Teams and business functions are interdependent and rely on the effective co-ordination of their work to achieve business objectives. Co-ordination does not necessarily mean increased centralisation or direct control. Irrespective of the size or complexity of a business, the key to effective co-ordination is information. For example, how do service delivery teams share information about their customers and the areas of work they are planning to develop? How can a business that has devolved responsibility for service delivery to regional groups ensure that minimum standards are maintained? How are managers, employees and other stakeholders kept adequately informed about what is going on? How well business activities are co-ordinated depends on how far its staff can obtain and process the necessary information.

Like most aspects of business, structure will depend on the particular circumstances – size, history, technology, the degree of uncertainty in the external environment – as well as on the values and culture of the business. Most businesses, regardless of size, have rules and procedures for referral and setting goals and targets. The formalisation of these procedures and standards, that is, the extent to which they are written down and made formal, will vary but will always be important. As we conclude this session, it is worth repeating that the ideas we have introduced here about business structure are not a set of levers that you pull to achieve certain automatic results. We have stressed that all structures have advantages and disadvantages and how they are implemented in a particular business setting will depend on how power is exercised generally and how decisions are taken. There is no right answer in such matters; the way work is organised and structured is always open to renegotiation.

3.5 Conclusion

This study session explored the structural dimension of businesses. There are important reasons for having a structure, not least so that everyone in the business knows what it is she or he is supposed to be doing. However, as in most types of organisation, the written down, or formal, structure does not tell us everything about how things may operate in practice. The informal structure of a business is about unwritten rules. This is the arena of culture which is the topic of the next study session in this book.

3.6 Learning outcomes

By the end of this study session on business structures you should be able to:

- identify and describe different types of business structure;
- describe the problems of the 'structureless' business;
- explain some of the dimensions or variables that could be used to explain the choice of structure within a business;
- outline some of the practical questions that arise when considering the structure of a business, for example, about the degree of specialisation and achieving co-ordination.

You will have developed your learning by:

- considering the notion of a business having no structure and the problems of trying to run such a business;
- appreciating the power of the informal structure of a business by applying it to a personal situation.

Session 4 Business cultures

Why are we studying 'business cultures'? Culture is a metaphor which can be used to explore the identity of a business. It is about how others see the business, but also how the individuals who work there understand it. Culture offers us a powerful insight into the business and what it is like to work within it.

The **aims and objectives** of study Session 4 are to:

- illustrate how the metaphor of culture can help us to understand more about the less obvious aspects of a business;
- demonstrate how the work of Hofstede (1980) on national cultures was used to develop the idea of organisational culture;
- provide some definition and explanation of the culture concept in the business context;
- consider some of the factors influencing or shaping culture.

4.1 National cultures

In study Session 1 we introduced a series of metaphors (Morgan, 1986) that provided some perspectives that we might use to achieve a different insight into business. One of these was the business as a culture, a type of micro-society where people work and 'live' together on a daily basis, with certain rules and understandings about what is acceptable and what is not. The idea of a business having a culture was developed from the work of Hofstede on national cultures (1980). His research focused on ways of measuring national culture and how these 'measures' might work differently in different contexts. The cultural values that are important in a national culture, he suggested, could be reflected in the way businesses within that country are operated and organised.

Hofstede's five dimensions (he developed four in 1980, then added a fifth in 1991) were:

Power distance   This concerns the extent to which less powerful members of organisations within a country expect and accept that power is distributed unequally. National cultures that demonstrated what Hofstede called a 'low power distance' are ones in which there is a concern to minimise inequalities. Hofstede included Sweden and New Zealand as examples of this. In general, Hofstede found that Latin American and Latin European (France and Spain) countries had higher power distance scores. The less powerful in these societies tend to look to those with power to make decisions, and inequalities within society are more acceptable. This is represented by a tendency for the centralisation of power and the subordination of those with less power within businesses.

Individualism/collectivism   In an individualistic society, people are expected to look after themselves and their families. In the case of business this is reflected in, for example, employment contracts based on hiring and firing. Two examples of countries with high scores on this dimension were

Australia and Canada. In more collective societies, people are more concerned for others and the culture is based around more cohesive groups, such as the family, which offer protection in exchange for loyalty. This tendency is reflected in businesses as well as elsewhere in society. Hofstede cited Ecuador and Indonesia as examples of more collective societies.

Masculinity/femininity   This refers to the degree to which gender roles are distinct and adhered to within a society. In high femininity societies, social gender roles overlap, with both men and women valuing 'feminine' qualities such as modesty, intuition and quality of life above the more traditionally 'masculine' qualities of aggression and competition. Hofstede's research suggested that Denmark and the Netherlands were more feminine cultures, while many other Western countries exhibited more masculine values. The USA was ranked fifteenth out of 53 nations on this masculinity score. Japan, the UK and West Germany also scored highly on masculine values.

Uncertainty avoidance   This concerns the extent to which the members of a society feel threatened by uncertain and unknown situations. Hofstede suggested that Jamaica and Singapore were relatively low uncertainty avoidance cultures, where precision and punctuality are less important, innovation is encouraged and people are motivated by being esteemed by, or belonging to, others above other things. High uncertainty avoidance scores mean that there is a fear of ambiguous situations, a preference for being busy and being precise and punctual. Relatively high scores on this dimension were found for Latin American and Latin European countries, Japan and South Korea.

Confucian/dynamism   This refers to the extent to which long-termism or short-termism appears to be the dominant approach. Long-termism stresses perseverance and being sparing with resources. Short-termism, in Hofstede's analysis, involves a greater emphasis on quick results. Hofstede found that the USA tended towards short-termism, while the Netherlands was the most long-termist European nation, ranked tenth out of 23 countries surveyed.

These differences between national cultures are based in deep-rooted values and so are largely implicit rather than openly acknowledged. They create all sorts of problems for employees in multinational companies who go to work abroad, or for representatives doing business with suppliers or customers in other countries. We can use the simple activity below to explore some of these differences.

Activity 4.1

Spend about **10 minutes** on this activity

Purpose: to consider business practices in different cultural contexts.

Task: consider each item in the following list. In your country's culture, is this behaviour considered to be acceptable or not?

- Paying an agent for an introduction to a business opportunity.
- Paying a government agent for bureaucratic procedures to be by-passed or speeded up.
- Making a copy of a product that you have seen at an international trade fair.

- Paying people to find loopholes in tax laws.
- Giving gifts to the purchasing manager in a large business organisation.
- Charging high interest rates for unsecured loans to individuals.

Feedback

Two people from two different cultures might give different answers here. One person might think that some of these behaviours were inappropriate or unethical, but the other might disagree. In some countries, these business behaviours could be against the law, but visitors might not know that, nor realise that they were offending the people with whom they were doing business.

The extract from a newspaper article in Example 4.1 provides insight into the problems of working abroad.

Example 4.1

Working abroad is often considered the chance of a lifetime. Living and working in a foreign country with all expenses paid; what more could anyone want?

In a surprising number of cases the answer is actually: 'Quite a lot'. Finding yourself adrift in a different culture might seem exciting when you're on holiday, but it's an entirely different proposition when you're living and working. Codes of business practice may be radically different and the expatriate lifestyle can be lonely ... yet many multinational companies have made little effort to prepare their employees for the shock.

The advertising giant J Walter Thompson is a case in point. 'We call in global relocation specialists to handle the practicalities of moving home and children's education,' says a company spokesman. 'But most other things we leave to the individual. The people we send abroad are experienced international businessmen and women and we expect them to understand different cultural milieus. There will always be the odd problem but we would hope that these could be dealt with by our local staff.' ...

But even with strong and knowledgeable support in the new country Chris Crosby, managing director of TMA, a company that specialises in corporate cross-cultural changes, believes more is required.

'Most people can identify explicit differences, such as clothing and food, which separate their culture from another and have little difficulty in adapting,' he says. 'More implicit differences are far harder to deal with. In the UK a business meeting is perceived as a place where a plan of action will be formulated and implemented. In other cultures, it is often just a forum for discussion. If you go abroad with the UK model as a preconception you might think that a meeting had been a disaster when it hadn't.' ...

'Rather than getting people to adopt a different culture than their own, you have to help them adapt their own style to a new culture. Critical to this is understanding one's own culture. Without examining our own underlying perceptions it is unlikely we will get to grips with another,' Mr. Crosby says.

But people are unpredictable and not all cross-cultural situations are cut and dried; many are ambiguous, so a key element of successful working practice is to concentrate on building relationships. 'Your job is to do the right thing for the business,' he says firmly. 'You need to be clear about non-negotiables, ethically and in terms of business operations.'

(Source: Crace, 2000)

Hofstede's work has had a major influence on how we think about the cultures of businesses in different countries. We understand that people expect different things and operate in different ways in business and other organisations because of underlying societal values. Hofstede's work provides valuable insights into what we might expect when we do business in other places; this is important information in a world of increasing globalisation. Of course, there are always exceptions to the rule. Some businesses succeed because of their very 'difference': individuals are often attracted to work for businesses that seem 'different', and some customers prefer to shop there.

'See? That means, "What do you clowns want?" '

Activity 4.2

Spend about **10 minutes** on this activity

Purpose: to reinforce understanding of culture in business.

Task: can you think of any examples where a business you have worked for, or heard about, has tried to operate in a slightly different way from what you would expect? List any examples you can think of and make some notes on how it looked or felt different, and why.

Feedback

The examples we thought of were the small, low-cost airlines which began to undercut the prices and operations of the large national airlines in the 1990s. They changed the whole way in which people think about international travel and make travel arrangements. Another example is John Lewis, the UK retail group, which calls all its employees 'partners'; all its employees have shares in the business.

This simple exercise was intended to get you to think about the less obvious things that make a business 'feel' different, and why potential customers and employees may or may not be attracted to them.

In the next section we begin to explore some academic definitions of this 'slippery' concept of culture at work.

4.2 Definitions of organisational culture

The cultural perspective has become popular in business studies because it offers a way of explaining performance and understanding difference. It is only one way of analysing business, but it is an interesting one as it focuses particularly on the insider point of view, or on what it is 'really' like to work in an organisation. There have been many definitions of organisational culture. One definition that is often cited is:

> Culture is a pattern of beliefs and expectations shared by the organisational members. These beliefs and expectations produce norms that powerfully shape the behaviour of individuals and groups within the organisation.

> (Schwartz and Davis, 1981, p. 33)

Another central idea about organisational culture is that it has to be learnt by newcomers and that it takes time to understand. The term *socialisation* is sometimes used to describe how new employees learn the less obvious rules about what is acceptable and what is not. An example of socialisation into a business is provided in Example 4.2.

Example 4.2

First opened in 1955 in Anaheim, California, Disneyland has been a consistent money maker for Walt Disney Enterprises. Most of those who apply for work at Disneyland are aware that if accepted on to the payroll they will be expected to conform to the large number of rules that are supposed to guarantee that the theme park is the 'Happiest Place on Earth'. In fact, ride operators and other hourly paid employees are a well-screened and fairly homogeneous group: white males and females, generally in their early twenties, of above average height, without facial blemish, and radiating good health. While ethnic minorities are employed, apart from their colour they tend to be close copies of the standard Disneyland employee.

Once in paid employment new recruits are enrolled at the University of Disneyland where they undergo a forty-hour apprenticeship programme. In the classroom employees learn about the history and philosophy of Disneyland, and the regulations and procedures that govern work there. Some of the most important of these concern the use of language. For example, employees are generally on first name terms, customers must be referred to as 'guests', rides are called 'attractions' and Disneyland itself is a 'park' not an amusement centre. At work employees are encouraged to think of themselves as 'back-stage', 'on-stage', and 'staging' and their uniforms as 'costumes'. Classroom instruction also covers approved responses to probable questions ride operators will face from customers, and how to summon assistance when accidents (always called 'incidents') arise or particularly difficult 'guests' cannot be mollified. The curriculum includes the inculcation of particular Disneyland values like 'the customer is king' and 'everyone is a child at heart when at Disneyland'. Great emphasis is also placed on checklists of appearance standards that must be learned, and which ban the wearing of facial hair, fancy jewellery or more than very modest amounts of make-up. Motivation levels are hyped by inspirational films, and pep talks exhort employees to be happy and cheerful while 'on-stage'. What is more, all relevant essential information is contained in a training manual, so no one can forget.

Informal socialisation mechanisms are equally well developed. New recruits soon learn that the job they are assigned to, the costume they are allocated, and the area of the park in which they work, determine their social status. Generally speaking the more highly skilled the work and glamorous the costume, the higher an individual's status. Employees also learn that there are strict limits to which the company line has to be taken seriously, and there is much satirical banter about the artificiality of Disneyland. Good performance on-stage is, however, a necessity. Individuals soon realise that supervisors are not just there to help them, but to monitor and evaluate their performance: most old hands can be counted on to relate tales of employees who have been fired for taking too long a break, not wearing part of the official uniform, or providing longer than usual rides. At the same time employees are taught by their peers how to get back at misbehaving 'guests' by tightening seat belts, slamming on the brakes unexpectedly, and drenching those standing on the banks of rivers. On the downside, although pranks are rarely played on newcomers, all are carefully scrutinised, and those deemed not to 'fit' are the subject of gossip and/ or ostracism.

The formal and informal socialisation procedures are not just fascinating to observe but commercially effective. Employees are generally willing to play the roles expected of them with good humour and kindly smiles, and this despite the fact that Disneyland does not pay well, the jobs require minimal intelligence and supervision is strict. Enculturation at Disneyland is thus a major feat of social engineering.

(Source: Adapted from Van Maanen, 1991, cited in Brown, 1995, p. 55)

How have academics and managers attempted to diagnose these largely hidden aspects of business? One well-known example is provided by Trice and Beyer (1984), who concentrated on the idea of there being symbols within a business. They divided these into, first, high-level symbols, which are the more obvious ones such as company buildings and logos, and, second, low-level symbols. They suggested four categories of low-level symbols: practices, communications, physical forms and a common language. These are explained below.

- *Practices* These are the rites, rituals and ceremonies of the business. These can take many forms, and would include the annual office party, employee awards and inter-site competitions.

- *Communications* These are the stories, myths and slogans that are circulated in the business. Stories about notable events in the past tend to become part of the culture of the business and can influence behaviour. How the business started, for example, or a period of particular success, can say something about preferred ways of performing and goals to aim for.

- *Physical forms* These include location, open plan or individual offices, types of eating areas, business suits or casual attire, flipcharts or whiteboards, and office furniture. For an interesting example go to the Google website and look at 'Inside Google' and 'Culture' in the 'About Google' area to see images of the culture and workplace at Google, the international internet search business. Also interesting are the 'Top 10 reasons to work at Google', which can be seen on the website and in the B120 Study Companion.

- *A common language* Jargon is common to many businesses. It is a convenient shorthand form of communication, but it also affects behaviour. Disney employees are 'cast members', while McDonald's employees are 'crew members'. The Open University is rife with acronyms: TMAs, TGFs, course codes like B120, and so on. This might suggest a rather technical and closed culture, but 'open and equal', the University's motto, is, in the experience of many of the staff, reflected throughout its business practices and values.

'After the merger, you may notice a few changes in our corporate culture.'

4.3 Factors influencing culture

Where the culture of a business comes from, and how it develops, is the subject of much discussion within business studies. Every commentator seems to have their own list of key factors. One example is by Drennan (1992), who proposes 12 key factors that shape the culture of a business. These are:

1   the influence of a dominant leader – the vision, management style and personality of the founder or leader in a business often has a significant influence on the values that the business tries to promote;

2   the history and tradition of the business – how things have always been done (and why);

3   the type of technology used by the business and the types of goods and/ or services it produces;

4   which industry or sector the business is in, and how much and what type of competition it faces;

5   the customers of the business – who they are and what they expect;

6   company expectations – based to a large extent on past performance;

7   the types of information and control systems used;

8   the legislation and wider business environment – as discussed in study Session 2;

9   the procedures and policies within the business – ever-evolving, but often a good indicator of underlying values;

10 the reward systems and the measurement of performance;

11 how the business is organised and resourced;

12 goals, values and beliefs – reflected in objects, actions and language, that is, in Trice and Beyer's symbols.

It could be argued that some of the 12 factors in Drennan's list are integral parts of the culture of a business rather than influences that shape it. You may, or may not, agree with this list, and it might be worth participating in a TGF discussion on the helpfulness of such lists. What lists such as this do show us, however, is that culture in business, as in society, pervades every aspect of its operations.

4.4 Conclusion

Culture is just one perspective that can help us to understand more about a business. In this section we saw how the concept of culture developed from research into differences between cultures at a national level. Many cultural elements of a business are not obvious, but there have been some attempts in the academic literature to develop definitions and identify influencing factors. It is possible to see, or 'feel', that one business is different from another, and that this involves more than just how it presents itself to the outside world. Business values and accepted ways of doing things are often reflected in a business's socialisation programmes.

In the next study session we move on to a topical aspect of business studies, business ethics.

4.5 Learning outcomes

By the end of this study session on business cultures you should be able to:

- explain the relationship between research on national cultures and the development of the culture perspective in business studies;
- describe some of the problems of working in, and doing business with, businesses in other countries;
- offer a definition of organisational culture;
- recognise the factors that constitute or influence the culture of a business.

You will have developed your learning by:

- accessing a website to explore, through visual means, the type of culture that exists in one particular business (Google) (see Section 4.2, 'Physical forms' paragraph);
- reading about other examples, such as the cultural training for employees at Disneyland.

Session 5 Business ethics

Why are we studying 'business ethics'? During recent years, a number of high profile scandals have cast the public gaze firmly on the way in which businesses conduct their affairs. People in business confront ethical decisions on a regular basis. The quality of their decision making has a significant impact on people inside and outside those businesses.

Business ethics is concerned with the study of how we ought to conduct business; the study of what makes certain actions within the business context the right, rather than the wrong, thing to do. When we use terms such as 'ought', 'right' and 'wrong' in an ethical sense, we are using them in a particular way.

The **aims and objectives** of study Session 5 are to:

- provide an understanding of what the study of business ethics involves;
- outline why an understanding of ethics is so important for business people;
- develop an appreciation of the different ways in which ethics relates to business;
- explore some perspectives on the relationship between business and society.

5.1 Defining business ethics

Consider Example 5.1.

Example 5.1

In the 1980s, many companies, including popular **brands** such as Ralph Lauren, Adidas, Gap and Nike, transferred manufacture of their products to developing nations. They did this because production costs were lower in these developing countries than in the developed world. In particular, it was cheaper to build factories and to employ people in countries such as Pakistan, Indonesia and South Korea than in Europe and the United States. However, media attention in the mid-1990s revealed that employment practices in these manufacturing plants left a great deal to be desired. Many European and American consumers were shocked to find that their expensive, branded clothing had been produced in unacceptable working conditions, sometimes even using child labour. This raised important ethical concerns among consumers and forced companies to rethink their production methods.

Ethics and values

First, let us evaluate the actions of these businesses without regard to ethics. In order to produce their shoes and clothing as cheaply as possible, it can be claimed that businesses ought to produce them in low-cost locations, using the lowest-cost labour. Looked at in this way, they were doing nothing wrong. In order to reduce costs and boost profits, employing cheap labour and spending as little as possible on factory hygiene and safety were the right things for these clothing companies to do.

However, when we use the terms 'ought', 'wrong' and 'right' in an ethical sense, we arrive at different conclusions. This is because ethics relate to values. The actions of these clothing businesses could breach values that are important to some of us. Most of us would agree that employing children, paying very low wages and expecting people to work very long hours in unpleasant conditions are wrong regardless of economic considerations. Businesses ought not to do these things, even if they enable cost savings and greater profits. Ethics, then, is about values.

Ethics and conflicting values

Another feature of ethics is that it tends to concern dilemmas. Issues such as dishonesty do not represent dilemmas for most people, because we all accept that they are wrong (but some people do engage in such practices even though they recognise that they are wrong). However, very few ethical decisions in business are so clear cut. It is a general feature of business decisions that they concern choices between alternative courses of action, all of which have advantages and disadvantages. Business ethics is no exception. Business ethics decisions usually present choices between competing value-based principles.

'I know nobody needs one – that's where the advertising people come in.'

Activity 5.1

Spend about **20 minutes** on this activity

Purpose: to think about ethical decisions in a real business situation.

Task: imagine that you work as a manager of a camp that runs adventure holidays for children. During their holidays, the children take part in activities such as rock climbing and canoeing under the direction of instructors who are employed by you. Observing strict safety standards is of paramount importance, since the lives of children and instructors are potentially at risk. You have been asked by your boss to consider introducing random drug and alcohol testing for instructors to ensure that their ability to fulfil their role is not impaired. Although your boss thinks that this is the right thing to do, she is leaving the final decision to you. While you can understand the reasons why these random tests should be introduced, you feel uncomfortable about treating your staff in this way.

Consider the following questions:

1   What conflicting values are at stake in this scenario?

2   What do you think would be the right thing to do, and why?

Feedback

On the one hand, as manager of the camp you will place considerable value on the safety of instructors and children. You will therefore feel that you have an ethical responsibility to do all that you can to ensure their safety. On the other hand, you may also place value on respect for the dignity of your staff. You may feel that asking instructors to submit to random drug testing is disrespectful to them and that it infringes their rights. Whatever course of action you choose, it will need to balance these competing values.

Ethics and the law

To a certain extent, the laws of any democratically constituted society define the ethical standards that are widely accepted within that society. They codify the values that a society holds dear, and therefore provide minimum standards of ethical conduct. However, many of the activities undertaken by individuals and businesses fall outside the scope of the law, yet still present ethical challenges. For example, there is no law against telling lies to a friend, although most of us would accept that to do so is unethical. Similarly, although there may be no law requiring businesses to adopt environmentally friendly policies or to refrain from using live animals for research purposes, most of us would agree that these are ethically charged subjects.

The businesses mentioned in Example 5.1 were breaking no laws, since they were acting in accordance with the laws of the countries within which they were manufacturing. However, many people considered them to be acting unethically. Therefore, although members of a society, or businesses that operate within it, have a responsibility to abide by its laws, it is clear that abiding by the law is not a complete recipe for ethical conduct.

Business ethics, morality and corporate social responsibility

Some other terms are often used in discussing business ethics: in particular, the terms 'morality' and 'corporate social responsibility'.

Morality

Some commentators make a distinction between the terms 'ethics' and 'morality'. However, everyday language, along with most of the business ethics literature, uses these terms interchangeably. In this session, for the purpose of clarity, only the terms 'ethics' and 'ethical' are used. However, in most cases the words 'morality' and 'moral' would serve the same purpose.

Corporate social responsibility

The term 'corporate social responsibility' (or CSR) was introduced in Section 2.3 of this book in relation to stakeholders. CSR is often used when discussing business ethics, particularly in the USA. Although CSR has a particular meaning when discussing the relationship between business and society, it is also often used to denote the subject of business ethics.

Ethics for all types of business

The realm of business is sometimes understood as the activities of profit-seeking, private enterprises. However, for the purpose of studying business ethics, such a definition of business seems too narrow. Many of the ethical challenges presented by business ethics, such as the treatment of people and interaction with the natural environment, are as important for public sector and non-profit making organisations, such as charities, as they are for commercial enterprises.

Business ethics: a definition

Business ethics, then, can be described as the study of how we *ought* to conduct business; the study of what makes certain actions within the business context the *right*, rather than the *wrong*, thing to do, from a *value-based* perspective. It often involves making *choices* between *conflicting values*. It is about *more than obeying the law.* And it is the concern *of all types of organisation,* not just profit-seeking, private companies.

5.2 Why is business ethics important?

Ethics is an often under-represented but crucially important subject for business people for a number of reasons. These include the following.

Businesses need to conform to the expectations of key stakeholders

Business success depends on the support of a number of key stakeholders. These include investors, customers, employees and suppliers. All of these stakeholder groups are becoming increasingly interested in the ethical performance of the businesses that they support. For example, many private investors will only purchase shares in businesses that meet certain ethical criteria. Customers are also becoming increasingly interested in ethical aspects of the sourcing and manufacture of goods. Businesses that have their own ethical codes will sometimes only do business with partners who observe similar standards. Furthermore, many people only wish to work for employers who conform to certain ethical principles. Therefore, in order to be successful, businesses must meet the ethical expectations of these key stakeholders. It is a task of business ethics to help business people to understand and respond to those expectations.

Business depends on society, so it must respond to the needs of society

Business and society are linked in a symbiotic relationship, which means that each depends upon the other. In our capitalist economy, business depends on society for its success and society depends on business success to ensure the affluence and material comforts that make life pleasurable. Business does not operate in a vacuum and business values cannot be separated from social values. It is a task of business ethics to help business people identify and respond to those societal needs.

Business can only operate effectively if certain norms are respected

Businesses can only operate effectively if those who take part in it follow certain common norms – or usual ways of doing things – and procedures. Businesses, and some individuals within them, may derive short-term gain from going against commonly accepted norms. In the longer term, however, businesses and those who work within them will only be successful if they observe shared standards of honesty, trustworthiness and co-operation. It is a task of business ethics to help business people define and understand these shared norms.

Business exercises considerable power over the lives of people

Business activity has a substantial impact on every person's life. For example, the way that products are made affects communities and the natural environment. The way in which products are marketed has a significant impact on how we think and behave. Furthermore, most of us spend a substantial part of our lives at work. The work environment has a massive impact on our quality of life, as do the financial and non-financial rewards that work provides. Therefore businesses, and business managers in particular, exercise considerable power over everyone's quality of life. It is reasonable to expect businesses to exercise that power in a responsible manner. It is a task of business ethics to consider what constitutes responsible use of the power that business wields.

Ethical behaviour has an intrinsic value

Most (although not all) ethical theories recognise certain objective values that make actions intrinsically right or wrong, irrespective of any instrumental considerations. Shared responsibility and blurred accountability within large and complex businesses may obscure these values and may encourage business people to disregard them. It is a task of business ethics to focus attention on those objective values and to encourage ethical accountability.

Example 5.2

The personal, social and economic consequences of the AIDS epidemic throughout the African continent are devastating. Although drugs to relieve AIDS are becoming increasingly available, their high cost precludes widespread distribution in Africa. In 1997, responding to the gravity of this situation, the then President of South Africa, Nelson Mandela, pioneered a law which gave his country the right to purchase large amounts of drugs overseas and sell them cheaply to his own people in order to fight HIV. But most importantly, the law also gave South Africa the right to 'compulsorily license' HIV drugs, permitting them to be produced more cheaply by someone other than the patent holder if this was considered to be in the public interest.

Clearly, the legislation introduced by Mandela was against the interests of the major drug companies of the world, who manufactured and sold AIDS drugs. These companies had spent millions of pounds and many years developing the drugs. The considerable investment that they had made in research and development was now to be undermined as these drugs were made and sold cheaply in Africa. They argued that Mandela's legislation would not only damage their profits, and thus their returns to shareholders, it would also impair investment in the research and development of improved drugs and possibly even an eventual cure for AIDS. Consequently, nearly 40 major European and American drug companies took legal action to protect their patents, declaring the action of the South African government to be in contravention of international law.

Legal proceedings lasted for nearly four years, attracting a great deal of publicity. The stance of the drug companies drew mounting criticism worldwide, notably from some pension funds that held large numbers of shares in these companies. Eventually, in 2001, the companies agreed to withdraw their action. Some are now actively exploring ways to make affordable AIDS drugs more widely available.

5.3 In what ways do ethics relate to business?

Ethical issues pervade all types of business in many different ways. Broadly speaking, ethics is relevant to business at three different levels.

1 The relationship between ethics and business at a macro level

At a macro (wide, strategic) level business ethics considers the overall framework within which business operates. You will remember the STEEP model in study Session 2 of this book. A key question at this level concerns whether government should intervene in business activity in order to pursue certain social objectives, or whether businesses should be left to run their own affairs.

2 The relationship between ethics and the social and environmental impact of business

Ethical considerations at this level relate to the impact of business activity on people, communities and the natural environment. Key issues include:

- Should businesses promote employment in local communities, or should they transfer production to cheaper overseas locations in order to make more money for shareholders and offer cheaper products to customers?

- Should businesses promote potentially harmful products, such as alcohol, tobacco and foods with high fat and sugar content, to vulnerable groups such as children?

- Should businesses actively promote environmental practices, such as using recycled raw materials or reducing environmentally damaging waste, or should they only focus on maximising profits and thus promoting shareholder wealth?

'We found someone overseas who can drink coffee and talk about sports all day for a fraction of what we're paying you.'

3 The relationship between ethics and the personal conduct of business people

At this level, business ethics considers the personal conduct of individuals in business. It asks how we should behave towards other people, be they colleagues, customers, partners or the general public. It focuses on issues such as treating people fairly, behaving in an honest and trustworthy manner and respecting people's dignity. In this respect, it has been claimed that the words 'business' and 'ethics' are mutually contradictory (Collins, 1994). Those who propose this view suggest that business is an inherently unethical enterprise, where lying, cheating and exploitation are all accepted parts of the game. However, few people nowadays would support this view. Most people inside and outside business accept that business people should conform to certain standards of ethical conduct and that the study of business ethics is a worthwhile activity that helps people to consider and define those standards.

5.4 What are the responsibilities of business?

Four broad perspectives have been adopted towards the role, or the purpose, of business in society. These are as follows:

1 The responsibility of business is to build shareholder value

The first perspective is that businesses exist for the purpose of maximising the wealth of shareholders. Therefore, business managers have a duty to maximise profits in order to maximise the wealth of owners. Nothing else counts.

2 The responsibility of business is to build long-term shareholder value

This perspective takes a more enlightened, longer-term approach than perspective 1 above. For example, it suggests that businesses will be more successful if they treat employees fairly, because employees will thus be more committed to the business and will work more productively. Similarly, businesses should build enduring, mutually supportive relationships with suppliers because this will be in the long-term interests of commercial success. Furthermore, businesses should adopt ethical policies that conform to the expectations of customers and other stakeholder groups because, without the support of these stakeholder groups, business would not be profitable in the long term.

Although this perspective encourages business managers to consider wider ethical considerations than the short-term shareholder value approach, the overriding principle is the same: that businesses exist for the purpose of maximising shareholder wealth. Business managers are expected to consider wider ethical issues insofar as these are consistent with building shareholder wealth in the long term. However, in the event of a conflict between long-term shareholder wealth and any other ethical considerations, the former should take precedence.

3 The responsibility of business is to respect the rights of a range of stakeholders

This perspective proposes that businesses have a responsibility to a wide range of stakeholders. These stakeholders include employees, customers, suppliers, local communities and, of course, shareholders. The multi-stakeholder approach also recognises the responsibilities that businesses have to conserve the natural environment. The difference between this rationale and perspectives 1 and 2 is that the multi-stakeholder approach holds that shareholders are only one of a number of groups to whom businesses have ethical responsibilities.

• Employees, for example, may develop firm-specific skills and forego other employment opportunities in the service of a particular business. Therefore, their interests are deserving of consideration by the managers of that business.

• Businesses benefit from special privileges, such as tax relief and government subsidies. They also make use of the resources of society. Therefore, businesses have a responsibility to respect the interests of society in general, not just the interests of shareholders.

4 The responsibility of business is to help to shape society

This perspective goes one stage further than perspective 3, the multi-stakeholder approach. It proposes that businesses should be proactive in supporting good causes. The argument is that business occupies an influential position in society. Therefore, in conducting its relationships with employees and communities and in marketing its products, a business should consider the positive and negative impact that it may have on society and should respond accordingly.

To help consolidate your learning about these four perspectives on the responsibilities of business, complete the following activity.

Activity 5.2

Spend about **1 hour** on this activity

Purpose: to reinforce your understanding of the four broad perspectives on the responsibility of business in society.

Task: read the scenario that follows and consider what response on the part of your business would be consistent with each of the four perspectives on the role of business in society.

In the early twenty-first century, a great deal of public concern, media interest and political attention in the West is focused on the subject of what we eat. Increasing obesity, particularly among the young, along with the linkage of heart disease and behavioural problems to diet, have fuelled concern with the amount of refined sugar, fat, salt and additives that are present in processed food. Imagine you are the marketing director of one the UK's largest food retailers. You are considering how your company should respond to the issue of healthy eating. Think about this in relation to each of the perspectives.

The responsibility of business is to:

1 build shareholder value;

2 build long-term shareholder value;

3 respect the rights of a range of stakeholders;

4 help to shape society.

Feedback

Perspective 1   If you adopted this perspective, it is unlikely that you would pay much attention to health concerns. You would consider the health of consumers to be their own affair. If consumers demand sweet, fatty food, with high levels of salt and additives, then your responsibility is to meet that demand. This will be the surest route to profitability and short-term shareholder wealth. However, if you adopt any of the other three perspectives, you will probably arrive at different conclusions.

Perspective 2   From this perspective, you may feel that, since society is becoming more concerned about the issue of health and diet, consumer tastes are likely to change eventually. Even if people want to eat sweet, salty, fatty food now, in a few years they will want more healthy options. Therefore, you should respond to this trend by making healthy options available now. Furthermore, being associated with healthy eating initiatives will reflect well on your company. Positive publicity as a champion of healthy eating may attract new customers, which will boost sales across your entire product range. It may also attract job applicants, giving you competitive advantage in the job market. Therefore, not only should you sell healthy food, you should also actively promote your support for healthy eating. You may wish to build on this image by sponsoring sports events and health initiatives. All these measures will boost revenue and profits in the long term, helping you to fulfil your responsibility to build shareholder value. On the other hand, you may take the view that healthy eating is just a passing fad or that it's not a big enough issue to justify any change in your policies. In this case, active promotion of healthy eating would be a waste of time and money. So your responsibility to build long-term shareholder value would be better served by carrying on as you are and selling just what consumers want.

Perspective 3   You may consider that the most important stakeholder right in this case is the right of customers to know exactly what they are buying. Therefore, you will ensure that all of the products that you sell clearly display information about ingredients. You may also feel that you have a responsibility not to encourage young children to consume unhealthy products. Therefore, you may reconsider how you market your products to children. You will also be aware of your responsibilities to other stakeholders. You will therefore need to balance your responsibilities to customers with your responsibility to shareholders, employees and creditors, all of whom have an interest in the commercial success of the business.

Perspective 4   You may take the view that healthy eating benefits society in general. Not only does it help people to live longer, happier lives, it also reduces the amount that we have to spend on health care and reduces the difficulties caused by behavioural problems. Therefore, you will do what you can to actively encourage healthy eating. You will use promotional and pricing initiatives to promote healthy food. You may also encourage research into healthy eating. You might even work alongside schools to educate children about the benefits of a healthy diet.

You may find that the courses of action proposed by these different perspectives do not conflict with one another. However, your rationale for adopting these courses of action differs depending on your view on the responsibility of business.

5.5 Conclusion

Business ethics is an important issue for everyone who makes decisions in all types of businesses. The effects of decisions and outcomes on individuals, stakeholders and the wider society must be considered. Academic research into the ethics of business is a growing area, and you will notice how many business news stories from around the world are prompted or influenced by an ethical dimension. We felt it was important to give space to a consideration of ethics in this introductory book. Often under-represented in mainstream business studies texts, ethics offers us another helpful perspective in our exploration of business.

In the next study session we begin to look at the different parts of a business, what they do and how they work together.

5.6 Learning outcomes

By the end of this study session on business ethics you should be able to:

- explain why business ethics is such an important area;
- describe how ethical issues relate to business.

You will have developed your learning by:

- applying what you have learnt to short business scenarios.

Session 6 An introduction to business functions

Why are we studying 'an introduction to business functions'? The different parts of, or functions, of a business create synergy, that is, a condition in which the sum of the parts is greater than the whole. Different functions are responsible for making different aspects of the business happen, but have to work together so that overall objectives can be achieved.

Business functions deal with different aspects of keeping the business profitable and sustainable and achieving business goals. Human resource management, marketing and distribution, for example, are separate functions, or parts of a business, but the activities and decisions in each will affect all the others, and there needs to be close collaboration and communication between the different functions. In this study session we present a brief description of each function, but it is important to always bear in mind that a business function cannot operate in isolation.

The **aims and objectives** of study Session 6 are to:

* provide an introduction to the business functions of human resource management, marketing, accounting and finance, operations and information management;

* describe the main activities within each function;

* demonstrate their impact and interdependence on each other.

6.1 Human resource management

The human resource management (HRM) function is responsible for all the activities concerned with the employment of the people within a business. It was, and is sometimes still, called Personnel, a name often associated with a very administrative and bureaucratic image. Despite this image, Personnel departments had their roots in a real concern for people at work and brought about some of the important changes in working conditions following the *Industrial Revolution*. The change to HRM was more than a change of name; it involved a wide, ongoing debate about different approaches to the management of people. However, many people object to the idea of people being just another 'resource' that a business uses to achieve its objectives.

The management of human resources does not, of course, happen solely within the HRM function; many individuals have to manage and deal with other people within a business.

Activities within the HRM function

Before we say any more about HRM, use Activity 6.1 below to reflect on what you might already know about this business function.

Activity 6.1

Spend about **10 minutes** on this activity

Purpose: think about the different activities within an HRM function.

Task: what do you know about the HRM function? Do you have personal experience of being an employee, at the 'receiving' end of HRM policies? Even if you do not have any work experience, have a go at making a list of the types of activities you would imagine an HRM department to be involved in.

Feedback

The HRM function is concerned with all aspects of managing people within a business. When someone joins a business, they enter into an employment contract, offering certain skills for agreed rewards and conditions. HRM deals with all parts of this employment contract, from the time it begins (recruitment and selection), through its ongoing maintenance and control (socialisation, performance management, job design, rewards, motivation), to the time either party terminates the contract (redundancy, resignation, dismissal, retirement).

We drew up the following list of examples:

- staffing policy and planning, drawing up contracts, and deciding how many and what type of people and skills are needed to help the business start/run/grow
- job design – who does what and how
- recruitment and selection
- induction and socialisation
- performance management – job appraisal
- motivation
- health and safety
- industrial relations
- training and development
- downsizing, redundancy, dismissal
- discipline.

Different businesses will give different prominence to the HR function, perhaps depending on their size and structure (see study Session 2) and organisational culture (see study Session 4). Small businesses do not necessarily have a distinct HR function, but the value of having a separate HR department, or representative, lies mainly in the objectivity they can bring to business processes such as selection and performance appraisal; that is, decision making that is not influenced by emotion or prejudice.

'We need to focus on diversity. Your goal is to hire people who all look different, but think just like me.'

6.2 Marketing

Marketing is the term given to the activities that occur at the interface between the business and its customers. The name comes from the concept of a marketplace, and marketing is concerned with matching what customers want to buy with what products or services the business is offering. The aim of marketing as a function is to ensure that customers will conduct exchanges with your business rather than with someone else's. Marketing is often associated with the negative image of getting people to buy things they do not want. Marketing practitioners, however, would argue that they have responsibility for ensuring that the customer comes first in the business's thinking.

Blythe (2005) suggests that the development of the concept of marketing was preceded by other business approaches, or philosophies. These were:

- *Production orientation*   During the nineteenth century it was believed that efficiency in the production process was the main way to succeed

- *Product orientation*   Rising affluence in the twentieth century meant people were not as prepared to accept standardised products. Businesses started to develop better and more specified products

- *Sales orientation*   As manufacturing capacity rose in the 1920s and 1930s, the supply of products could outstrip demand and so the activity of actively selling became more important. This is the view that customers will not ordinarily buy enough of a product without an aggressive selling and advertising campaign

- *Consumer orientation*   Modern marketers take the view that customers know what they want and recognise value for money. They will not buy from the business if they feel that are not getting what they want. This is the basis of the marketing concept; putting the customer at the centre of the business.

A more recent development is ***societal marketing***, which means that marketers should take some responsibility for the needs of society at large and for the sustainability of their production activities. Customers are increasingly concerned about the ethical (see study Session 5) and environmental (see study Session 2) factors associated with business and their products.

Activities within the marketing function

Effective marketing is based on a good understanding of how consumers behave and make decisions. There is a need to identify gaps in the market and anticipate opportunities. One way of describing what employees in the marketing function do is to say that they deal with the 'marketing mix', first introduced by McCarthy (1987). McCarthy described this mix as the four Ps of marketing: product, place, promotion, price.

Product The product should be what the customer wants and expects to get.

Place The product should be available from wherever the target group of customers finds it easiest to shop, whether that is a high street shop, door-to-door delivery, a catalogue, or online shopping.

Promotion All communications about the product should be put across in a way that will appeal to target customers.

Price The product should always be seen as representing good value for money. Customers are usually prepared to pay a bit more for products of better value.

The growing importance of the provision of services prompted an extension of the model. Blooms and Bitner (1981) added another three Ps, to make the 7-P framework.

People Virtually all services are dependant on the people who perform them, so people are, in a sense, an integral part of the product the business is offering.

Process Services are usually carried out with the customer present, so the process by which the service is delivered becomes part of the product.

Physical evidence Almost all services contain some physical evidence: the hairdressing salon produces a haircut, the fast food chain produces a burger, the accident and emergency department in a hospital produces a prescription or plaster cast.

It is important to think of the 7-Ps as a mix. One ingredient cannot be substituted for another; each must be added in the right form and quantity.

As well as understanding their local or national market, marketing people need to be aware of international and cultural differences in factors such as customers' preferences and how goods and services are promoted.

6.3 Accounting and finance

Finance, or money, is an important resource for all businesses. The financial aims of a private-sector business will include making a profit. In the public sector, the main objective will be to make the best use of financial resources.

The accounting and finance (A&F) function is responsible for communicating appropriate financial information to internal and external stakeholders (see study Session 2), many of whom will not be financial experts.

'So what if I underestimated costs and overestimated revenues? It all averages out in the end.'

Activities within the accounting and finance function

The detailed activities of the A&F function will vary in nature from the operational to the strategic, that is, from costing future plans to calculating actual income and expenditure, and will be influenced by the external environment of the business. The nature and purpose of the accounting and finance activities carried out within a business fall into two main categories, *management accounting* and *financial accounting*, although there is overlap between the two. A description of each is provided below.

Management accounting information is produced for *internal* consumption. It is financial information for the managers of a business for such purposes as:

- *planning* and *budgeting*
- *management control* and *operational control*
- performance evaluation
- making decisions about particular activities, tasks and functions
- making decisions about *investment and disinvestment.*

Financial accounting provides information for people *outside* of the business: for example, external stakeholders such as shareholders, investors, suppliers, providers of *loan capital*, government, electors, competitors.

The purposes of financial accounting include:

- external reporting
- providing information to allow resource providers to make choices about investing in the reporting organisation
- disclosures about stewardship (how resources entrusted by a person(s) have been managed on their behalf by the person(s) making the disclosure)
- disclosures that facilitate public accountability

- encouraging competition by making information available to competitors.

Financial management involves the raising and spending of capital finance by a business. The financial reports and accounts produced by the A&F function contain essential information about profit and loss, balance sheets and cash flow. The annual report and accounts of a business provide financial stakeholders with information about the business in which they have invested. Ongoing internal communication about the financial position of the business is essential to managers, decision makers and, indirectly, all employees.

6.4 Operations

The operations part of a business can best be thought of as the activities that produce the goods and/or deliver the services required by its customers. This function is often seen as a transformation process, changing inputs into outputs. The success of any business is related to its ability to manage its operations efficiently, to make the best use of resources, and to meet the requirements of its customers effectively. As the 'doing' part of the business, operations is central to achieving the business's aims. It is responsible for producing the goods, or delivering the services.

There is often a misconception that operations management is concerned only with manufacturing activities. Although much of the academic study of operations management does have its origins in the manufacturing industries, many of the key concepts are equally applicable to services. The distinction between manufacturing and services is, in many respects, artificial and increasingly irrelevant. Service transactions do have distinctive characteristics. They may, for example, be intangible: you cannot store a haircut. But, from the point of view of operations management, even the most basic product will have some element of service accompanying it. Conversely, most services have some tangible product as an integral part of what is delivered to the customer. A hairdresser stocks and sells hair products, for example.

In business studies, operations is often given less attention than other functions, yet operational activities are a major component of business. The next activity, based on an essential reading from Capon (2004), conveys some key learning points about operations.

Activity 6.2

Spend about **2 hours** on this activity

Purpose: to establish a greater understanding of some of the key terms and activities within the operations function within business.

Task: read and make notes on Essential Reading 3, 'Operations' by Capon, which is at the back of this book. Practice your note-taking skills by making a clear, concise list of important points about the role of operations.

This essential reading was intended to give you a more detailed introduction to the operations function in a business. It shows the breadth of operations and the key role it plays in any business. The principles of operations management can be applied to both manufacturing and service organisations. This activity is also designed to develop your skills of reading and note taking.

6.5 Information management

There are three important points to note about information management (IM). First, IM is a *conscious* process; it does not just happen, but should be based on planning. Second, the purpose of IM is to assist in *decision making*. Information is gathered to be used in the business and, therefore, is most useful when the starting point is the decision to be made, with information following from that. Third, the definition highlights that IM is for the benefit of *all levels* of a business, and should be about aiding decision making for all, not just those in senior management positions.

The IM function is concerned with all aspects of managing information within businesses. As the business changes over time, business processes and information systems need to be built and maintained. Every business function has a role in these activities, but the information management function has a more active role because many of the processes and systems incorporate information and communications technology (ICT). People often confuse information management (IM) with the management of ICT. While ICT is one of the central tools of the information management function, it tells only part of the story.

Activities within the information management function

Information management has the capacity to bring about change in almost all business processes and is critical to much of the innovation that takes place. This is because information and communication technologies can manipulate, analyse and transport information in a host of new and creative ways. The increasing use of ICT by the customers of a business – for example, searching for information and products, online banking and shopping – means that the IM function has to think about both internal and external communication and information systems. The security of both business and customer information then becomes a major concern.

'I'm sure there are better ways to disguise sensitive information, but we don't have a big budget.'

6.6 Cross-functional issues

Dividing business functions, and businesses themselves, into separate categories can help us to analyse them, but it can be misleading. We need to understand not only the purpose and main activities of each business function, but also the interdependence between them. No business function exists in isolation, and people who work in one functional role will have 'customers' in other functions, as well as in other businesses. For example, a maintenance engineer in a factory will have the production team as his customers.

To end this study session you will visit the virtual world of a small business environment to look at their business functions, what they do and how they work together.

Activity 6.3

Spend about **1 hour** on this activity

Purpose: to develop your internet skills and consolidate your understanding of business functions.

Task: go to http://www.bized.ac.uk and click on the 'virtual worlds' icon at the top. Then go to the 'virtual factory'.

Have a (virtual) look around the graphical representation of a small business, a hot air balloon factory. Short descriptions of what happens in each business function are provided at the click of a mouse! Make notes if you wish, but the main aim is to consolidate your understanding of business functions via an alternative, online learning resource.

Feedback

You will have noticed that research and development (R&D), a business function we have not covered in this session, was included in the virtual company on the website. R&D is a crucial part of many businesses.

6.7 Conclusion

In this study session we looked at the different functions that make up all businesses, albeit on different scales. We provided introductions to human resource management, marketing, accounting and finance, operations and information management. While, for the purposes of analysis, we looked at each of these separately, we stressed that they are all interdependent parts of a whole. What happens in one business function will always have implications for all the others. Finally, we looked at some of the functions in action, working together, using a virtual example.

6.8 Learning outcomes

By the end of this study session on business functions you should be able to:

- describe the main activities within each business function;
- explain the interdependency of business functions on each other and on the outside world.

You will have developed your learning by:

- reading and taking notes on Essential Reading 3 about operations management;
- navigating access to the Biz-ed internet site and exploring the business functions within a virtual small business.

Session 7 Small business and entrepreneurship

Why are we studying 'small business and entrepreneurship'? Small businesses make up about 98 per cent of all business activity within the UK, with similar figures across the European Union. It is the entrepreneurial skills and spirit of individuals that create businesses and make them a success.

The arena of the small business is often understated, or even completely ignored, in business studies courses. This is a serious oversight, as in many countries most of the workforce is employed in the small to medium sized enterprise (SME) sector. SMEs make an important contribution to the wider business environment and to the lives of their employees and consumers. In the UK, for example, of 2.3 million jobs created by new businesses between 1995 and 1998, 85 per cent were in small businesses (Kirby, 2003).

The **aims and objectives** of study Session 7 are to:

- describe the importance of the small business sector in a national and international context;
- construct a definition of what is meant by a small business;
- explore some of the issues faced by family businesses;
- examine how small businesses may arise and the vital role played by entrepreneurial behaviour;
- introduce the types of help that are provided to encourage and sustain the small business.

7.1 The benefits of the small business

The SME sector plays a major role in creating employment, and new jobs ultimately impact on business activity through increasing spending power. Other benefits to the wider economic and social life of a society include the following.

- SMEs can offer specialised services to customers that larger businesses may not regard as cost effective to provide. Small businesses often work as sub-contractors on big projects being managed by larger companies.
- SMEs are likely to have specialised knowledge of the local business environment and can tailor their products and services appropriately.
- In contributing to the local infrastructure, SMEs assist in regional and local growth and rejuvenation.
- Smaller businesses may be able to innovate in ways that larger ones would find difficult. They tend to be less bureaucratic and more flexible in their response to customer demands.

7.2 Defining small and medium sized enterprises

Activity 7.1

Spend about **30 minutes** on this activity

Purpose: to search the internet for some definitions of 'small business'.

Task: there have been various attempts to define what constitutes a SME. Your task is to complete the definitions of the following terms:

Self-employed =

Micro business =

Small business =

Medium sized business =

Large business =

To start this task, take a look at the European Commission's definition of three of these terms. You can find the definitions by selecting an internet search engine such as Google, Yahoo! or MSN. Search the web, rather than just pages from the UK, and enter the phrase 'the new SME definition' into the search terms box. The search results should locate a document with this title in pdf format.

Having noted these definitions you can then search for definitions of the other two terms – you could also look for further definitions of micro, small and medium-sized businesses.

Feedback

In addition to using the number of employees in a business, other criteria could include levels of profits, annual sales (turnover), type of ownership, organisational structures and market share.

7.3 Where do small businesses come from?

One of the obvious starting points for a small business would be the individual who comes up with an idea for a product or service for which he/she believes there is a market. This might be a completely new product, such as James Dyson and his bag-less cyclotron cleaner, or it might involve taking an established product or service and doing it better or differently, such as EasyJet in the case of low cost flying.

The impulse might come from someone who is made redundant from their job and who decides to use this opportunity to try self-employment. This is referred to as a 'push factor': someone is pushed by circumstances into trying something new. Or there could be a 'pull factor' at work. Here, the personality of the individual makes it difficult for them to work for someone else. They don't like to be given orders, and the bureaucratic hierarchy of big business cannot contain their need for independence. In other words, they are pulled along by their drive and personality. There could, of course, be a combination of push and pull factors. In the deep recession of the 1980s, for example, many individuals in the UK were made redundant from traditional industries such as mining and sought to start up their own small businesses. The fact that they were pushed does not mean there was no pull.

There is also the possibility of a management buy-out, starting on a small scale, leading to the creation of a new small business. This might arise because the owners decide to sell a part of an existing business. Or individuals might move into small business ownership through the purchase of a franchise, buying a local outlet of an existing and, often, proven idea for a product or service. This reduces some of the risks connected with a small business start-up: market research has already been undertaken, training is provided, and the product or service is already known and has a track record. However, there is still the problem of finding the personal capital to fund the purchase. The more established and successful the franchise, the more expensive it will be; for example, some of the McDonalds or Body Shop outlets.

Influencing factors on the creation of a small business are likely to be: the perceived opportunity and availability of assistance; and the perceived attributes and resources of the individuals concerned (Bridge et al, 2003).

Other motives for starting up a small business could include:

- an individual's prior experience: strong interests or hobbies and/or work experience;
- being a member of a minority ethnic group: a small business can be a way of 'entering' mainstream society on one's own terms and breaking through barriers to employment;
- level of education: self-employment may be the way forward for those who left formal education at the earliest opportunity (perhaps because they could not fit into the hierarchy and constraints of school life), or, indeed, for very well educated people with particular skills or knowledge;
- exposure to role models: in many cases the *entrepreneur* has come from a family where entrepreneurial activity is present. Founder of the Body Shop Anita Roddick's parents ran their own business.

7.4 The risks involved

The risk of personal loss often acts as a barrier to those who wish to start up in business. There is usually no guarantee that your product or service will capture a share in the marketplace; market share has to be won in a competitive business environment. First, you must find start-up capital from somewhere – savings, redundancy money, family or friends – and this may be lost if the business fails. Even if you have a little personal capital, you may need to borrow on top of this, and the lender will normally require security, that is, a guarantee that if things go wrong with the business there will be a way of repaying the loan by the sale of *assets*. Would you be prepared to use your house as security on a loan for a business idea that has not yet been proven? Many do, and that is perhaps what contributes to them being considered entrepreneurial; they are risk-takers. Then, in the early stages of the new business income may be low, or even non-existent, as you meet start-up costs such as paying for your stock and employing others.

Other barriers that may hinder the creation of a new business are:

- a lack of knowledge about the opportunities and support for entering self-employment;
- a lack of role models within the society and/or within the family of those who have set up their own businesses.

The Osmonds, a very successful family business in the 1970s

The example below about family businesses is an extract from a *Financial Times* article and forms the basis for Activity 7.2 which follows immediately after. Look at the activity 'task' before reading the example.

Example 7.1

A family business is often seen by outsiders as having particular drawbacks, such as family members who hang on to the business to support their lifestyle. But being family-owned can bring benefits beyond the thrill of having your name over the door.

'There are some good business reasons why a family owned company might want to stay family owned,' says Peter Leach of the Stoy Centre for Family Business. 'A family business can use its "family-ness" to create competitive advantage and differentiate itself from its rivals.'

For many families, the values embedded in the business keep them from selling out to a much bigger company that would swallow them up. 'Pride in their family's achievement is strong and there is often an overall sense of stewardship. The last thing most owners want is to be seen as the generation that sold the family silver,' says Grant Gordon, director-general of the Institute for Family Business, an independent association of family businesses.

But, as Mr Leach warns, the emotional ties must not be allowed to override commercial realities. 'Families often want a legacy with their name on it, or they argue that they have to keep going because their business creates local employment. These are emotional reasons and can be dangerous. The business must be run on proper lines.'

Deciding whether you are maintaining your family business for the 'right' reasons is not always simple. Mr Leach recommends that families constantly challenge why they are there, what family ownership brings to the company and whether it has a long-term future. 'You have to free yourself of the emotional stuff and challenge the status quo. It is about the constant updating and articulation of why you have a family business,' he says.

Staff employment is one issue. 'It is really important to a lot of families that they are seen to be promoting progressive employment and they see the family ownership paying off in terms of motivation and enterprise,' says Mr Gordon. He says family firms have a commitment to their staff that goes beyond what is expected of, say, a multinational, and can reap rewards from that.

A potential benefit of family ownership to the business is 'patient capital': shareholders who do not demand an ever-increasing monetary return. However, family business advisers warn that paying a decent return on family holdings may be necessary to avoid damaging family arguments.

'Many family businesses are able to take a much longer-term view than publicly quoted companies,' says Mr Gordon. 'The stock market can be an unfriendly place. Family businesses can take unorthodox business decisions with a view to building a business that might not make money for years to come but has lasting value.'

But taking the long view requires agreement and commitment from all the owners: in a family business there is a danger of failure because a fragmented ownership cannot agree on the purpose of the business, or the best means of achieving it. If the business has a large number of minority shareholders, a common vision may be difficult to formulate and the business may need to work hard to build a family creed to bring owners together. 'You need inspired leadership, a family leader who has fire in his belly,' says Mr Gordon.

But this may be a problem, Mr Leach says. 'To be honest, it's the minority of family businesses that have a good gene pool. Later generations are usually not as good as the first and you should bite the bullet if you believe you should sell.'

Succeeding generations may find the necessary drive by changing the nature of the business, which can anyway be an important factor in maintaining it. William Jackson & Son, the Hull-based food company, which makes products such as Yorkshire pudding under the brand name

Aunt Bessie's, is now in the fifth generation; it started as a corner shop and the company moved into insurance and motor dealership before returning to its roots.

Another family concern, Timpson, has likewise changed, moving from shoe manufacturer to shoe retailer to shoe repairer and most recently diversifying into watch repairs.

John Timpson, chairman and chief executive of the Timpson's chain of 330 shoe repair, key-cutting and watch repair shops, feels passionately about the company started by his great-grandfather. 'Never a day goes by but I think about something to do with the business,' he says. 'It is my number one hobby – I have to be careful not to drive the rest of the family mad.'

Alexander Hoare, the first so far among the 11th generation of the family to join the privately owned bank C. Hoare, is also motivated by emotional ties. 'There is a sentimental attachment. The family business does generate some quite powerful forces and those forces can be good for the business – they can be a useful recruitment and retention tool among family members. A lot of people are motivated by more than money.'

But he also sees direct advantages for customers. The bank keeps customer numbers at a level that allows decisions to be taken on the basis of personal knowledge. 'We were recently able to lend a customer £1m at 24 hours' notice, without having to go through several layers of credit checks. That would have been very difficult to arrange in a publicly owned bank – the controls and bureaucracies wouldn't allow it.'

The personal touch in family businesses extends to managing staff. Mr Timpson plans a big party for staff next year to celebrate the business's centenary, which will be held at his home. 'People have met me and my son [James, managing director], they feel they know us and they like that,' he says. 'They know who is running the business and who is going to run it. That continuity is tremendously powerful. How can a business run well if the CEO is changed every three years'

But he also cites other reasons why family ownership is beneficial. 'We can make terribly quick decisions. We just do it – and don't have to worry about calling a board meeting. And there is a lot less politics. There's no one breathing down my neck.'

A large number of family owners at C. Hoare (eight family members are involved in management) ensures that strategy decisions are a group affair. But family ownership allows that strategy to follow an unusual path. Mr Hoare says: 'It is nice to be able to offer something that the other banks cannot. We are deliberately positioned somewhere completely different to our competitors. There is an exceptional level of service and that is one of our specialities.'

The enthusiasm and emotion that drives a family business can overcome problems that would cause other companies to go under and extract a level of commitment for which multinationals would pay a lot of money. But it must be tempered with commercial and practical sense.

(Source: Gascoigne quoted in Capon, 2004, pp. 34–5)

Activity 7.2

Spend about **50 minutes** on this activity

Purpose: to find out more about family businesses, a common type of small business.

Task: read Example 7.1. As you read, make notes on possible advantages and disadvantages of family ownership of a business.

Feedback

Capon suggests the following advantages and disadvantages of private family ownership of a business.

Advantages	Disadvantages
• 'family-ness'	• emotional ties may override commercial sense
• greater motivation and enterprising drive	• no agreement over the purpose of the business
• no outside shareholders seeking ever increasing monetary gains	• later generations may not be as enterprising
• less organisational politics	
• greater flexibility	

Example 7.2 offers further insight into some of the issues of working in a family firm.

Example 7.2

When Paolo Gucci, the grandson of Gucci's founder, wanted to launch his own label in the 1980s, his family stood in his way. In revenge, he exposed his father's personal tax evasion to the US authorities. His father ended up in jail and Paolo was exiled from the business, living out his days, broke, on an English farm. In the mid-90s, Paolo's cousin Maurizio, who owned the lion's share of the firm, wanted his cousins out of the business, so he teamed up with an investment firm in an effort to buy them out. Then, in a repetition of history, his cousins informed the police of his shady tax records and Maurizio took off to Switzerland to avoid arrest. The Gucci family later lost complete control of the brand. Family businesses have long been associated with their fair share of scandal and emotional baggage, with ugly spats frequently ending up documented in lurid newspaper headlines ...

…

For women, a family business may offer job security, flexibility and support when it comes to having children. Marcelle Metta gave birth a month ago and together with her sister and mother runs the UK franchise of the Paul & Joe boutiques. 'I can completely rely on my family to keep me informed about what's really going on while I'm not there. There is absolute trust between us,' she says …

…

Disagreements between family members are of course inevitable. 'There were times we had to take it outside the shop as customers came in while we were rowing,' admits Marcelle Metta, 'but now our roles are carefully defined, each of us works more independently and we delegate more. We've learned to create boundaries and to suggest alternative solutions rather than apportion blame. Sometimes people have to make their own mistakes and then discover it for themselves.'

…

Mannie Sher, principal organisational development consultant at the Tavistock Institute, warns of the risks of joining family businesses. One big reason for their breakdown, especially in the third generation, he says, is family members failing to prepare for future leadership and being unable to relinquish control …

Yet Rotary Watches chairman, Robert Dreyfuss, whose siblings are shareholders though not employees, says, 'There's something magic about a family business.' Dreyfuss firmly believes the heritage of this fourth generation family company affects the bottom line. 'Our greatest competitive advantage in a world of huge, faceless corporate conglomerates is that we are a family business – ours is a team effort, not a bureaucracy'.

(Source: Adler, 2005)

7.5 Entrepreneurship

Entrepreneurship is the activity of entrepreneurs, people who create new products, processes, services and markets. Entrepreneurs often develop new ways of working and doing business. Research carried out in the UK proposed some key motivational aspects for would-be entrepreneurs. In order of significance, these were:

- more freedom
- make money
- be my own boss
- gain more respect
- dissatisfied with job
- need a job

- more of a challenge
- lead and motivate others
- family tradition
- being at the forefront of technology
- been made redundant
- implement an idea or innovation

(Shurry et al., 2002, p. 41)

These results were based on responses from 1,746 entrepreneurs, or would-be entrepreneurs.

A great deal of research activity has taken place to try to determine why some individuals are more entrepreneurial than others. This includes trying to answer questions about why some people are more comfortable about taking risks. Results suggest that certain characteristics underpin entrepreneurial behaviours and that these often arise from a combination of psychological and socio-economic factors. Work in the 1960s by McClelland (1961) and others has since been critiqued and built upon, but some of the key ideas are still important in a consideration of the nature of the entrepreneur.

McClelland suggested that an entrepreneurial individual has:

- a high need for achievement, a drive to excel. This is often reflected in strong commitment to a work ethic, where the individual is prepared to work the long hours often necessary in starting and running a business in its early days, and is able to persevere when the going gets tough;
- the tendency to be a risk-taker. This does not necessarily mean that they will rush into something, but rather will show the ability to calculate the degree of the risk;
- the ability to cope with and tolerate ambiguous situations, where decisions have to be made but the information may not be complete;
- the need for personal autonomy: they want to be in charge of the business. They do not fit well within rigid hierarchal structures;
- a high internal locus of control. In other words, they have a high belief in themselves, believing that they are in control of their destiny;
- an ability to be open to and spot opportunities as they arise. Entrepreneurs are said to be opportunistic. In this sense, they may be outward-looking and creative in non-conventional ways. They may have an approach that would challenge acceptable norms of business behaviour.

Activity 7.3

Spend about **10 minutes** on this activity

Purpose: to reflect on your personal thoughts about, or your experience of, a small business.

Task: reflect on the following questions:

1   Which of the risks outlined in Section 7.4 would be the most worrying to you personally?

2   Do you recognise any of McClelland's personality traits of an entrepreneur as being like you?

Feedback

While we have been considering entrepreneurship in terms of the characters of individuals, it is important to bear in mind that we are all shaped by our upbringing, education and experiences. Setting up a business will be less of a step into the unknown for some people than it will for others.

7.6 Support for the small business start-up

Lack of information about the opportunities available was cited in Section 7.4 as one of the possible barriers to starting up a small business. From the 1990s to 2007, a government agency, the Small Business Service, was in existence in order to support these organisations, aiming to:

- champion a culture that prizes and fosters enterprise, and help businesses start and develop as their capabilities grow

- make sure that government support services (including access to finance) are accessible, relevant and of high quality

- make special efforts to release the enterprise of ethnic minority groups, women entrepreneurs and others who have such potential to contribute to UK business.

(Small Business Service, 2005a)

This agency was subsequently renamed the Enterprise Directorate in 2007, under the central government Department for Business Innovation and Skills (BIS), with a similar remit.

> The Enterprise Directorate aims to boost enterprise, start ups and small business growth by helping small and medium businesses to start and thrive through:
>
> - Improved access to finance.
> - A more positive business environment: which supports growth and ease of starting a business, and where new businesses and economic opportunities are more evenly shared between regions and industries

- Better and more targeted business support
- Building a more entrepreneurial culture, equipping people with the skills and ambition to start a business.

(Department for Business Innovation and Skills, 2010)

If you are interested in finding out more about the SME sector, you may wish to visit the Enterprise Directorate website (http://www.bis.gov.uk/ policies/enterprise-and-business-support), or use a search engine such as Google to find support services for the small business sector in the country in which you live.

7.7 Conclusion

It has been possible within this study session to give you only a brief insight into small businesses and entrepreneurial individuals. You should, however, have been able to identify the significant role these play in the modern economy and business arena. The small business is a distinct type of organisation with distinct needs. Bridge et al. sum this up nicely:

> Understanding both small businesses and their place in an economy requires [therefore] more than an understanding of businesses in general. It requires an appreciation of the significant differences between small and big businesses, a knowledge of specific small business issues, and an insight into the ways of small business. It also requires an understanding of the entrepreneurs who start and run small businesses.

(Bridge et al., 2003, p. 229)

7.8 Learning outcomes

By the end of this study session on small businesses and entrepreneurship you should be able to:

- offer a definition of a small business;
- describe some of the motives behind, and barriers against, starting a small business;
- discuss some of the characteristics of the entrepreneur.

You will have developed your learning by:

- accessing a website and acquiring up-to-date information about small business. You may also have found out about other websites supporting small businesses in other regions or countries;
- reading and making notes on examples of family businesses.

Conclusion to Book 1

In this first book of B120 we introduced a number of different ways in which we might approach the question, 'what is a business' We provided an introduction to some of the key topics within the business studies literature, such as stakeholders, structure and culture, as well as reading about some often under-represented areas such as business ethics, the operations function and small businesses.

We explored some different perspectives, or ways of seeing business: for example, metaphorical, ethical and cultural approaches, as well as well-known business techniques such as the SWOT analysis and the STEEP model.

We stated at the outset that B120 will not cover all aspects of business studies, nor provide detailed descriptions of each area of study. The purpose of Book 1, and of the course generally, is to introduce some important and interesting ideas about business, and to emphasise that business does not just involve the large, Western corporations that we tend to hear about the most. The aim of this course is to highlight the great variety of business and the impact it has on all aspects of our lives.

We hope you have enjoyed Book 1 and that you have taken advantage of all the support that studying with The Open University provides. We are sure that by now you will be familiar with the power of your online TGF as a learning tool. Not only can it offer additional insights and alternative answers, it also provides a place for collaborative learning and moral support. Throughout the course, use your Study Companion, your tutor, your fellow students, the online resources and the examples and activities in the course books to your best advantage. All these elements combine to make up B120, and your learning, study skills, enjoyment and knowledge of business will be enhanced if you use them to the full.

We hope you enjoy the rest of the course.

References

Adler, C. (2005) 'Office hours: are you reliant on the family business?', *Guardian*, 11 April.

Blythe, J. (2005*) Essentials of Marketing*, 3rd edn, Harlow, Prentice Hall Financial Times in association with The Open University.

Booms, B. H. and Bitner, M. J. (1981) 'Marketing strategies and organisation structure for service firms' in Donnelly, J. and George, W. R. (eds) *Marketing for Services*, Chicago, IL, American Marketing Association.

Bridge, S., O'Neil, K. and Cromie, S. (2003) *Understanding Entrepreneurship and Small Business*, 2nd edn, Basingstoke, Palgrave Macmillan.

Brown, A. (1995) *Organisational Culture*, London, Pitman.

Capon, C. (2004) *Understanding Organisational Context: Inside and Outside Organisations*, 2nd edn, Harlow, Prentice Hall Financial Times, Pearson Education Limited.

Collins, J.W. (1994) 'Is business ethics an oxymoron?', *Business Horizons*, September – October, pp. 1–8.

Crace, J. (2000) 'Feel at home with a job abroad', *Guardian*, 14 October.

Department for Business Innovation and Skills (2010) *'Enterprise & Business Support'* [online] http://www.bis.gov.uk/policies/enterprise-and-business-support (accessed 06 October 2010).

Drennan, D. (1992) *Transforming Company Culture*, London, McGraw Hill.

Freeman, J. (1972–3), 'The tyranny of structurelessness', *Berkeley Journal of Sociology*, Vol. 17, pp. 152–3.

Hatch, M. J. (1997) *Organization Theory: Modern Symbolic and Post-modern Perspectives*, Oxford, Oxford University Press.

Hofstede, G. (1980) *Culture's Consequences: International Differences in Work Related Values*, London, Sage.

Kelso, P. (2005) 'Football: Burns urges radical reform', *Guardian*, 11 June.

Kirby, D. (2003) *Entrepreneurship*, Maidenhead, McGraw Hill.

Lilley, R. (2003) 'Doing the business', *Guardian*, 2 April.

McCarthy, E. J. (1987) *Basic Marketing: A Managerial Approach*, 9th edn, Homewood, IL, Irwin.

McClelland, D. (1961) *The Achieving Society*, Princeton, NJ, Van Nostrand Reinhold.

Morgan, G. (1986) *Images of Organization*, Beverly Hills, CA, Sage.

Pugh, D. and Hickson, D. (1968) 'The comparative study of organizations' in Pym, D. (ed.) *Industrial Society*, Harmondsworth, Penguin.

Schwartz, H. and Davis, S. (1981) 'Matching corporate culture and business strategy', *Organizational Dynamics*, Summer, pp. 30–48.

Shurry, J., Lomax, S. and Vyakarnam, S. (2002) *Household Survey of Entrepreneurship: Research Report for Small Business Service*, London, Department of Trade and Industry.

Small Business Service (2005a) 'About the SBS' [online] http://www.sbs.gov.uk/ (accessed 26 February 2006).

Small Business Service (2005b) 'Government action plan for small businesses' [online] http://www.sbs.gov.uk/ (accessed 15 March 2006).

Trice, H. M. and Beyer, J. M. (1984) 'Studying organizational cultures through rites and rituals', *Academy of Management Review*, Vol. 9, pp. 653–69.

Essential Reading 1
Analysing stakeholders

The analysis of stakeholders involves identifying who they are and considering their power and interest with regard to the organisation. Stakeholders can be identified by brainstorming and shown on a stakeholder diagram – see Figure R1.1. Once identified, the relative power and interest of the stakeholders can be mapped onto a power and interest matrix – see Figure R1.2[1]. Additionally this analysis can be extended to consider the reaction behaviour and position of stakeholders if a particular strategy or plan were to be implemented by the organisation.

Figure R1.1 Stakeholder diagram

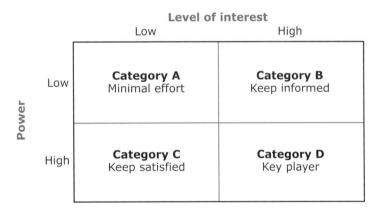

Figure R1.2 Power and interest matrix

Source: Johnson, G. and Scholes, K. (1999) *Exploring Corporate Strategy*, 5th edition, Prentice Hall Europe.

Stakeholders with high power and high interest (category D)

Stakeholders with high power and high interest are key players in the organisation and are often involved in managing the organisation and its future. If key players are not directly involved in managing the organisation, it is vital that they are given serious consideration in the development of long-term plans and the future direction of the organisation, as they have the power to block proposed plans and implement their own alternative agenda.

Stakeholders with high power and low interest (category C)

Stakeholders with high power and low interest are those who must be kept satisfied, for example institutional shareholders. Institutional shareholders will often remain compliant while they receive acceptable returns on their investment and are pleased with the organisation's management and activities. However, the ability of category C stakeholders to reposition themselves on the power and interest matrix into category D and become stakeholders with a continuing high degree of power and an increase in their level of interest should not be under-estimated. This occurs when category C stakeholders are not kept satisfied and feel that their interests are not being best served. Hence stakeholders with high power and low interest will increase their level of interest to make sure that their interests are met. The shift in position of unsatisfied category C stakeholders may impede an organisation's plans and prevent the expectations of key players or category D stakeholders from being met as expected.

Therefore a canny organisation will ensure that the expectations of category C stakeholders are well met and the necessary adjustments made to meet changing expectations arising as the current issues facing the organisation change. This helps ensure that category C stakeholders do not feel that their interests are being marginalised at the expense of the interests of key players, category D stakeholders. Hence the repositioning of category C stakeholders should not be an unexpected occurrence if they are managed appropriately. This requires a good working relationship and open channels of communication to be developed between category C stakeholders, the organisation and key players or category D stakeholders.

Stakeholders with low power and high interest (category B)

The stakeholders in category B are those with low power and high interest, who are able to exert relatively little power in influencing the organisation and its actions. However, these stakeholders have a high level of interest in the organisation and will voice their concerns if that interest is not being considered in a suitable manner. If category B stakeholders voice their concerns loudly enough and in the right way, e.g. via lobbying or petitions, they may be able to influence one of the powerful group[s] of stakeholders in either category C or D and affect their behaviour. Therefore organisations need to keep category B stakeholders informed of the organisation's activities and decisions and in doing so convince them that their interests are being taken into account and considered seriously.

Stakeholders with low power and low interest (category A)

Stakeholders with low power and low interest are those in whom the organisation need invest only minimal effort. However, category A stakeholders should not be ignored as they may acquire a stake in the organisation by becoming, for example, a customer, supplier or competitor, which will mean an increased level of interest and/or power.

The Automobile Association and its stakeholders

It should be recognised that the position of stakeholders on the power and interest matrix is dynamic and will vary over time according to the current issues that the stakeholders are considering. The situation in which the Automobile Association (AA) found itself during April 1999 provides a good example of an organisation with groups of stakeholders who line up in a certain way due to a particular issue, in this case demutualisation.

The AA was founded in 1905 and by 1999 held around half the motor breakdown market, a market that was experiencing significant change. These changes included the acquisition of Green Flag by Cendant, the entry of the insurance company Direct Line into the market, and the RAC's expected trade sale or flotation. Therefore in April 1999 the AA considered its options with regard to retaining its mutual status or demutualising. It was rumoured that Ford had informally approached the AA with a takeover offer that would end the latter's mutual status. Other interested bidders were thought to include Centrica and a number of venture capitalists. The then Director-General of the AA, John Maxwell, initiated a strategic review to allow the AA to assess its options. The options available included demutualisation, a joint venture with a suitable partner or takeover by another company. The merchant bank Schroders was advising the AA.

In 1999 the AA had annual sales of around £600 million from its businesses, which included roadside service, publications and driving schools, and its value was estimated to be between £1 billion and £1.5 billion. Pursuit of the demutualisation option and stock-market flotation would give each full member of the AA a moderate windfall of £200–250. In 1999 the AA had 9.5 million members, of which 4.3 million were full-paying members who would receive the windfall payouts. However, excluded from the demutualisation windfall were the 1.7 million associate members, including the families of full-paying members who benefit from the association's services, and the 3.5 million members who are drivers of fleet cars with AA cover and drivers who received their AA membership as part of a package when purchasing a car.

The AA and stakeholders with high power and high interest (category D)

The key players were the Director-General of the AA and his immediate management team carrying out the strategic review, as well as the full members of the AA – see Figure R1.3. John Maxwell and his management team were key players with high power and high interest, as their planning and decision making would determine their future with the AA, the future of the AA, the future of those who worked for the AA, and the future of AA members. The full members would collectively decide whether the AA was to demutualise. They might have chosen to support any demutualisation recommendations made by John Maxwell and his team, or to reject them in favour of a bidder, such as Ford, buying the AA. The full members, for example, might have decided this if they were to lose confidence in John Maxwell and his management team and their ability to carry out the demutualisation successfully ...

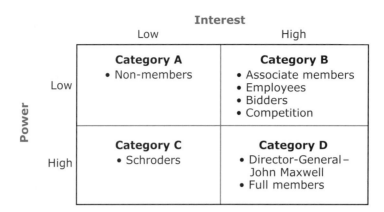

Figure R1.3 Power and interest matrix for the Automobile Association (AA)

The AA and stakeholders with high power and low interest (category C)

The merchant bank Schroders was a category C stakeholder, as it had relatively little interest in whether the AA finally decided to demutualise. However, while in the position of corporate adviser to the AA, it was relatively powerful as it was able to advise and potentially influence John Maxwell and his management team.

The AA and stakeholders with low power and high interest (category B)

The category B stakeholders, those with high interest and low power in the demutualisation issue, included associate members and employees. The associate members clearly had a high interest in whether or not the AA decided to demutualise. The primary concerns for associate members were the effect of demutualisation on the services they received and the cost of associate membership. However, as non-voting members, associates had no direct power to influence the outcome of any ballot on demutualisation. Equally, employees had a high interest in the future of the AA and would be concerned as to the effects of demutualisation. Potential effects of demutualisation could have included the AA becoming more competitive and this being achieved via cost cutting and job losses. However, employees had no direct role in the ballot and would ultimately have to accept its outcome.

The stakeholder matrix suggests that category B stakeholders, high interest and low power, have to be kept informed, which is true of stakeholder groups such as associate members and employees. In April 1999, the AA kept its members and employees informed by issuing the following statement to the media and via answerphones in its own offices:

> The AA has always kept an open mind about its structure as it pursues its prime purpose: to serve the best interests of its members. No decisions have been made in this respect.

However, also with high interest and low power were other stakeholders like potential bidders such as Ford and competitors like Direct Line and Green Flag. These were external stakeholders with a great deal of interest in what the AA would eventually decide to do, as their business and the marketplace in which they operated would be directly influenced by that decision. Any organisation should be aware that any information it releases with the intention of keeping stakeholders such as employees and associate members informed will be in the public arena and therefore available to stakeholders such as competitors and potential bidders.

The AA and stakeholders with low power and low interest (category A)

The category A stakeholders are those with low power and low interest. For the AA, non-members fell into this category. They were unable to receive breakdown services from the organisation and had no influence over its demutualisation decision. However, it should be recognised that stakeholders' power and influence can alter over time. The opportunity of a £200–250 windfall might have encouraged some non-members to become members and move to category D, high interest and high power. This was perfectly possible, as the AA made it clear that it was not closing its doors to new members, nor was it expecting to distinguish between long-term and short-term full members:

> The AA has no intention of bringing the shutters down on membership. Everyone is as free to join the AA as they were before[2].

> There is no distinction made among full members[3].

If the number of new full members joining had been very large and there was no differentiation between new and longer-term members, the value of the windfall paid to full members could have decreased. This could have pushed longer-term full members to seek to lobby or influence John Maxwell and his management team to distinguish between long- and short-term members.

Stakeholder alliances and coalitions

When analysing stakeholders, two points should be noted. First, people and organisations may belong to more than one category of stakeholder. Second, stakeholders and organisations may depend on one another, with the nature of the dependency varying according to the amount of power and/or interest the stakeholder has in the organisation. For example, if the Director-General of the AA favoured demutualisation, he would have depended on the full-time members voting in large enough numbers for the demutualisation proposals. However, he would have needed to recognise that full members might have been subject to influence by associate members, who may have been related to full members, e.g. husband and wife. Similarly, some employees (category B) were also full members of the AA and how they were treated and informed as employees might have influenced their voting behaviour as full members. The employees might have felt that cost cutting and job losses were likely to result from demutualisation. Hence they might have lobbied and sought to influence the voting full members to vote against a change in the AA's structure or to vote for a takeover rather than demutualisation if they thought their best interests would be served in this way. Equally, if associate members were concerned about the service they received and its cost, they might have sought to influence full voting members, which would perhaps have been easy if the full voting members were family members. In addition, associate members and employees might have sought to influence John Maxwell and his management team directly, via letter-writing campaigns and petitions.

Therefore the arguments in favour of demutualisation had to focus on the benefits for full members (cash windfall and service levels at least maintained, preferably improved in some way), associate members (service levels at least maintained, preferably improved in some way), and employees, particularly those who were also full members (issues of job security and future operation of the AA for employees were crucial).

The members of the AA were balloted in August 1999 on the proposed sale of the AA to Centrica. The result of the ballot was announced in mid-September 1999 and showed 67 per cent of eligible members voted and 96 per cent of them voted in favour of the sale. The sale to Centrica was completed in July 2000 for £1.1 billion.

References

1 Johnson, G. and Scholes, K. (2002) *Exploring Corporate Strategy*, 6th edn, Harlow, Financial Times/Prentice Hall.

2 Jagger, S. (1999) 'AA ponders its road to the future', *Daily Telegraph*, 24 April.

3 Ibid. [Jagger, S. (1999) 'AA ponders its road to the future', *Daily Telegraph*, 24 April.]

(Source: Capon, C., 2004, *Understanding Organisational Context: Inside and Outside Organisations*, 2nd edn, Harlow, Prentice Hall Financial Times, pp. 387–92.)

Essential Reading 2
Strengths, weaknesses, opportunities and threats

Strengths

A strength is a competence, valuable resource or attribute that an organisation uses to exploit opportunities in the external environment or to help it counter threats from the external environment. Strengths could include a resource such as a well-motivated and skilled workforce, with low turnover, or an attribute such as a strongly established brand image or reputation. Examples include Cadbury's Dairy Milk brand and Marks and Spencer's reputation for good quality.

Stakeholders and key success factors

Customers are stakeholders in an organisation and fulfilling *key success factors* involves the organisation in meeting the needs and expectations of its customers and other stakeholders … For example, a key success factor may be a good relationship with a reliable supplier. This will be especially true if the supplier is the only supplier or one of very few supplying a key component or part. Meeting the key success factors will require the organisation to meet the supplier's expectations, which will include regular orders of a certain minimum size, with little room for negotiation on price if the supplier is powerful.

In seeking to satisfy stakeholders, especially customers, while at the same time outperforming competitors, organisations should seek to:

- fulfil the key success factors for the industry or market;
- develop competencies that provide competitive advantage (see discussion on competitive advantage and premium prices);
- utilise competencies to meet the requirements of specific customers and aim to charge a premium price.

Competitive advantage and premium prices

Competitive advantage arises from the unique features or 'extras' that a product or service possesses and for which customers are prepared to pay a higher or premium price. For example, some dry cleaners offer a standard service and a gold service. The standard service includes dry cleaning the item of clothing, pressing it by machine and returning the item to its owner on a cheap hanger with a polythene cover over it. In contrast, the gold service includes dry cleaning the garment, hand pressing and finishing it before it is returned to its owner on a more robust hanger and in a more substantial plastic cover. There will be a small group of customers who will be prepared to pay a higher or premium price for the extras that the gold service provides. Being able to offer the gold service will give the dry cleaner a competitive advantage over nearby dry cleaners who do not offer this service.

Weaknesses

A weakness is defined as lacking a competence, resource or attribute that an organisation needs to perform better than its competitors in the external environment. A company producing tableware for the domestic and catering markets will rely in part on styling and designs to make products appealing to customers. If it relies on the designs that have always been used or occasionally on shopfloor staff coming up with new patterns, it is likely to lack competence in design, a key success factor for the tableware industry. The lack of a key resource, such as a new piece of technologically advanced equipment, is also a weakness, particularly if your competitors have access to that equipment.

Opportunities

Opportunities are openings or chances in the external environment or marketplace that an organisation may pursue to obtain benefits. The identification of a new geographic market in North America for a firm's products is an opportunity. Such opportunities can be exploited by manufacturing the product in the firm's home country and exporting it to North America, or by forming a strategic alliance with a local US company and having the benefits of the greater understanding of the local and national external environment offered by that partner in the strategic alliance. This type of arrangement will also need to confer benefits on the alliance partner, otherwise it is unlikely to be successful in the long term. The third alternative is to manufacture the product locally, which is perhaps the most time and resource consuming of the three options as it involves setting up from scratch in a foreign country. This will be more difficult than operating in a home environment or with advice from an organisation for which the foreign market is a home environment.

Key success factors

The degree to which an organisation is successful depends on its ability to meet its key success factors (KSF). Key success factors are what an organisation must do well and better than its competitors if it is to succeed. They can arise from a number of sources.

First, key success factors may be established by the industry in which an organisation operates. For example, in the clothes mail-order business, being able to provide speedy delivery to the customer's home is a key success factor for all companies in the industry. Second, key success factors may be determined by the organisation itself. When the Midland Bank set up telephone banking with its subsidiary First Direct, the key success factors were to provide an accurate banking service that required a minimum amount of paperwork, could be accessed 24 hours a day, and did away with the need for high-street branches. Other banks have adopted these key success factors by providing their own telephone banking services and will continue to try to meet these key success factors by providing banking services in the home via the internet.

Finally, key success factors may be signified by customers indicating that they require products with particular features or services. One example is the demand from consumers for high-quality take-away coffee from coffee bars and sandwich shops. The demand from consumers is not only for high-quality coffee but also for a range of different types of coffee, from the familiar cappuccino and espresso to the more exotic sounding café latte, mocha and arabica. Therefore a key success factor for coffee and sandwich bars is the provision of a wider range of high-quality coffees.

Threats

Threats have the potential to damage an organisation's performance in the marketplace or external environment. Threats often arise from competitors or factors that are outside the control of the organisation. The competitor that cuts prices by 50 per cent today and the competitor that brings out a new generation of technologically advanced products both pose a clear threat to all other organisations operating in the same industry. Threats may also arise from changes in legislation or taxation relating to the industry in which an organisation operates. For example, the imposition of value added tax (VAT) on newspapers and books or children's clothes would affect both the manufacturers of such products and the amount of business done by retailers selling such products to members of the public.

Clearly, threats from the external environment may endanger an organisation. However, threats may also jeopardise good opportunities of which the organisation expects to take advantage. In 1997 the US company WorldCom tendered £19 billion for MCI, another US company. This offer outbid BT's proposal of £11 billion for MCI by over 70 per cent. The WorldCom offer became a realised threat that snatched an opportunity from under BT's nose and left a gap in the latter's strategy to secure a global partner.

Different types of SWOT analysis

The most basic SWOT analysis will examine how threats and opportunities can be dealt with while allowing the organisation to utilise its strengths and weaknesses to meet its key success factors [objectives]. ... Lists should be brief and specific, indicating the key and important issues. The threats, opportunities, weaknesses and strengths should be judged and assessed in relative terms. For example [a strength or opportunity in relation to how a competitor fares with the same] ... Organisations need to aim to be better than competitors when it comes to possessing strengths and exploiting opportunities. The same holds true for weaknesses and threats: organisations need to seek to minimise the effect of these to a greater extent than their competitors.

A basic SWOT analysis should ... include an assessment of where the company is at the current time and where it wishes to be at some point in the future. The organisation also needs to decide how far away that future is – it will vary from a few months to many years depending on the organisation, the nature of its business and its current situation.

Guidelines for carrying out SWOT analysis

...

Strengths

Decide whether the organisation has the appropriate strengths on which to build and exploit its opportunities. How can it best exploit its strengths in relation to the opportunities available to it? Which strengths should the organisation seek to develop for the future?

Weaknesses

Decide whether remedying weaknesses is more urgent than building on strengths to exploit opportunities. Does ignoring important weaknesses make the organisation vulnerable to threats which could result in its going out of business or being taken over? How can critical weaknesses be offset or converted into strengths?

Opportunities

Identify new markets and market segments that might be suitable given the organisation's existing strengths and competencies. Identify changes that are occurring to existing customers and within existing markets. Consider using strategies of market penetration and market development to take advantage of any opportunities arising from existing and changing markets ... Identify changes that need to be made to products and services. Consider strategies of product development and diversification to take advantage of any opportunities arising from changes to existing products ...

Threats

Do threats need managing more urgently than the opportunities pursued? Which threats need to be dealt with immediately and in the short term? Which threats are issues for the organisation to consider when undertaking longer-term planning? How can critical threats be offset or turned into new opportunities?

(Source: Capon, C., 2004, *Understanding Organisational Context: Inside and Outside Organisations*, 2nd edn, Harlow, Prentice Hall Financial Times, pp. 393–7.)

Essential Reading 3
Operations

Introduction

Operations management is the term applied to the activities at the core of any organisation's business and is concerned with the way in which the organisation actually puts into practice what it has set out to do. An organisation will undertake operations to make a product, provide a service or perform a combination of the two. Hence Glaxo manufactures pharmaceuticals; BT provides telecommunications services; and Laura Ashley produces and sells clothes. Accordingly, operations management is concerned with managing the way products are made and/or service delivered, which has a direct connection with how the organisation achieves its objectives. The principles of operations management can be applied to any organisation.

Organisations and operations management

On comparing and contrasting two very different organisations, it would appear that their operations have few similarities. The operations of Glaxo, for example, would seem very unlike the operations of a chip shop run by its self-employed owner. However, closer examination will reveal surprising similarities. Both organisations have to choose the best location, buy raw materials, forecast demand for their products, calculate the required capacity, arrange resources to meet demand, use the raw materials to make products, sell the products to customers, manage cashflows and human resources, and seek out reliable suppliers. Both Glaxo and the chip shop want to run an efficient operation, with high productivity.

There are two basic ways of categorising organisations and the operations they undertake. The first is to consider organisations as belonging to different sectors: primary, secondary or tertiary – see Figure R3.1. Primary-sector organisations are concerned with producing raw materials and include oil extraction, coal mining, diamond mining and farming to produce food. Secondary-sector organisations manufacture and produce goods, often from raw materials produced by primary-sector organisations. Tertiary-sector organisations sell goods produced by primary and secondary organisations. The tertiary sector includes service-sector organisations such as banks and social services.

...

Primary	Secondary	Tertiary
Farm Cereals (wheat, barley) ———→ Meat (beef, lamb, pork) ———→ Cattle (milk) ———————→	Bread baked —————————— Burgers and sausages made —— Butter and yogurt produced ——	→ Baker sells bread → Butcher sells burgers and sausages → Grocer sells butter and yogurt
Oil company Crude oil ◄	→ Petrol distilled ————————— → Lubricants/oil distilled ———— → Plastics manufactured ————	→ Petrol station sells petrol → DIY store sells oil for squeaky door → Plastic sold to manufacturer of car bumpers
Coal company Coal —————————————	→ Smokeless fuel produced ———	→ Local coal merchant sells smokeless fuel to domestic customer

Figure R3.1 Manufacturing and service sectors

An alternative way of viewing organisations is to consider whether the organisation produces goods, provides a service or delivers a mixture of both, and whether it is a private-sector organisation or not – see Figure R3.2 for more details. There are no public-sector/not-for-profit organisations that manufacture. If a public-sector or not-for-profit organisation is to provide a manufactured product, it is most likely that manufactured goods will be made by a subcontractor from the private sector. For example, local councils provide domestic and commercial council tax payers with wheelie bins which are not manufactured by the council but bought in bulk via a negotiated contract from a supplier in the private sector.

	Not-for-profit organisations	Public-sector organisations	Private-sector organisations
Manufacturing			• Pharmaceuticals (GlaxoSmithKline) • Cars (Vauxhall) • Food (Northern Foods)
Manufacturing and service	• Retailing (Oxfam shop/fair trade initiatives)	• Housing associations (build and let homes) • Provision of artificial limbs (NHS)	• Restaurant (Pizza Hut) • Retailing (Laura Ashley) • Carpet shop (supply and fit carpet)
Service	• Charities (Red Cross) • Religious organisations (Church of England)	• General practitioner (GP–NHS) • Refuse collection (local council) • Education–schools (LEA)	• Banking (Abbey National) • Telecommunications (BT) • Hotels (Hilton)

Figure R3.2 Manufacturing and service organisations

Operations management

Operations management … is concerned with forecasting the output required and scheduling the conversion process such that customers' orders are delivered on time. …

The principles of operations management … can be applied to organisations providing a product, service or mixture of both. …

First, we consider the service and product organisations. The most basic difference between a service and a product is that a product is tangible – the car can be touched and driven by the customer – whereas a service is intangible – the financial advice cannot be seen and touched. The latter is delivered by the financial adviser and assimilated by the customer simultaneously and cannot be stored to be repeated another day. This contrasts with a product, which is able to be stored, highlighting the delay between manufacture and consumption. For example, the car is built in the factory and there will be a delay of at least a few days, maybe longer, before it finally reaches the customer who is going to own and drive the car.

The level of contact that occurs between a service provider and customer and a manufacturer and customer is also very different. In delivering a service there is significant contact between the service provider, the financial adviser, and the customer; in contrast, the buyer of a good, such as the purchaser of a car, and its manufacturer are very unlikely to have any contact at all. This is because in providing a service the customer is part of the process of its delivery: the customer has to be there to receive the financial advice. Therefore the facilities are located close to the customer, e.g. the bank's office will be on the local high street and accessible to the individual receiving the financial advice. In contrast, the customer will not participate in the manufacture of their car and the factory is likely to be located some distance from the end user, maybe even in another country. Finally, in general services are labour intensive and production is automated.

An organisation that both provides a service and delivers a product will assume characteristics of a service provider and/or a manufacturer. Taking the example of a pizza restaurant, the food is a tangible product, but cooking and serving the food are intangible services. The food may have been stored in the restaurant's fridge or freezer before being used to produce a pizza. Serving a meal is a service that cannot be stored and indicates the simultaneous nature of service provision: the food is served hot as soon as it has been cooked and is eaten as soon as it is served. Showing the diners where to sit, giving them menus, taking their orders, serving the food and taking payment are all service provision and will therefore involve contact between the waiting staff and customers in the restaurant. In contrast, there will be limited or no contact between diners and the kitchen and cooking staff who produce the pizza. Again, as a service is being provided, the location will be easily accessible to diners: pizza restaurants are on the high street in most towns in the UK. The dining area of the restaurant will be the section of the premises most accessible and used by diners; the storage areas, kitchens and bins will be towards the back of the premises and rarely accessible to customers. A restaurant is one example where providing the service, done by the waiting staff, and production, food preparation and cooking, are both labour intensive.

...

Location

An organisation deciding on a location will have to consider a number of alternatives. The best location for a manufacturing organisation may be one where the overall costs are minimised. In a service organisation the customer is directly involved in the supply process, therefore issues such as ease of access and speed of delivery have to be considered along with costs.

...

Product development

Product development and forecasting are both activities that occur early in the operations management process. The commercial evaluation of a new product will include assessing or forecasting likely demand. ...

To be successful, an organisation has to manufacture the products that customers desire. Therefore it must discover the kind of products that customers require and continue to supply them. To do this an organisation has to introduce new products and update or withdraw old products from the market ... The development and introduction of a new product are expensive activities, hence careful planning is essential ... [see] Figure R3.3.

...

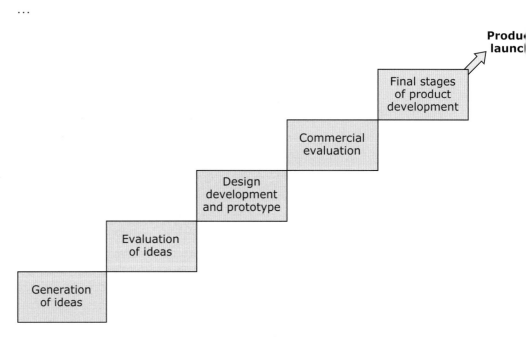

Figure R3.3 Product development process

Forecasting

Forecasts become effective at some point in the future when a decision is made concerning, for example, demand for a product. Hence forecasts need to be based on the likely conditions in the future. In the example of a company trying to predict demand for a product, conditions such as the amount of disposable income consumers will have and the competition's activity will affect the forecast. For instance, a company manufacturing ice cream making a forecast in December concerning demand for ice cream in the following June, July and August will consider the likely weather conditions and the new varieties of ice cream to be launched by its competitors for the summer.

There are a number of ways in which forecasting can be done. One key criterion for a forecast is the time period in the future that it covers.

…

Forecasting can be either qualitative or quantitative in nature. Quantitative or numerical forecasting is feasible if the company is already producing the product or providing the service, as historical data already exists concerning the demand for a product or service and the factors affecting demand.

… Qualitative methods of forecasting rely on the views and opinions of different stakeholders.

…

Layout of facilities

Facility layout is concerned with the physical arrangement of resources in the organisation's premises. It covers all types of organisations, for example factories, offices, schools, shops and hospitals. The location of resources and their location with respect to other resources is important – if done well, the flow of work is smooth and efficient; in contrast, poorly laid-out facilities disrupt operations and reduce efficiency.

The layout of resources in an organisation therefore has two clearly linked aims: to organise the resources and facilities so that the desired output of product or throughput of customers is achieved using minimum resources, and to ensure that the physical arrangement of resources allows maximum output or throughput. Consequently the layout and design of an organisation's premises should allow operations to run efficiently.

…

Process and system performance

All organisations have a finite capacity: a factory can manufacture only so many TV sets in a month, and a school can accept only a finite number of new pupils into Year 1 every September. Therefore consideration at the design stage of the process system is needed to determine the capacity required in order that products can be made, or services can be offered, to meet the demand of customers.

System capacity involves a significant capital investment, hence careful planning should be undertaken to optimise the utilisation of financial resources and meet demand. This can be crucial, as customers can be lost quickly if a firm's capacity is insufficient to meet demand. Alternatively, under-utilised capacity can be very costly. For example, a local education authority will close down a school if pupil numbers fall significantly, as maintaining school buildings and employing staff are costly activities.

Defining capacity and measuring performance

In theory, an organisation examines the forecast demand for a product and from this determines the capacity needed to satisfy that demand. However, in practice factors other than forecasted demand affect capacity, for example how hard people work, the number of disruptions, the quality of products manufactured and the effectiveness of equipment.

Capacity is a basic measure of performance. If a system is operating to capacity, it is producing the maximum amount of a product in a specified time. Decisions concerning capacity are made at the location and process design stage of an organisation's operations management activities. Ideally, an organisation should aim for the capacity of the process to match the forecast demand for products. Mismatches between capacity and demand will result in unsatisfied customers or under-utilised resources. If capacity is less than demand, the organisation cannot meet all the demand and it loses potential customers. Alternatively, if capacity is greater than demand, the demand is met but spare capacity and under-utilised resources result.

In contrast, if the capacity utilisation hovers around 100 per cent during certain time periods, then on those occasions bottlenecks or queues will occur. A common example of capacity being less than demand is when you are left standing in a long queue in a sandwich bar at lunchtime. You may exercise your consumer choice and go to another sandwich bar with no queues and many staff waiting to serve you. Here capacity is greater than demand, but the cost of paying these under-employed staff will be reflected in your bill.

…

Process flow charts

The activities, their order and relationship between activities can be shown in a process flow chart. For example, the process a customer goes through when visiting the hairdresser is examined. The operations carried out at the hairdresser's might be described as:

- junior sweeps up hair clippings;
- pay receptionist;
- arrive on time and tell receptionist you've arrived for appointment;
- junior makes you a cup of tea or coffee;
- make next appointment;
- hair is cut by stylist;
- hair is washed by junior;
- you look in mirror and confirm you are happy with haircut;
- wait for stylist to finish cutting previous client's hair;
- sit down and read magazine until called;
- hair is dried by junior.

…

Drawing up a process flow chart will help answer the following questions:

- What operations are performed?
- What is the sequence of these?
- Which operations cannot be started until others have finished?

- How long does each operation take?
- Is the system being used to full capacity?
- Are products being moved?

Once the process flow chart for a product or service has been drawn up and the basic questions above answered, areas for improvement in the process can be looked for and examined.

In the example of the visit to the hairdresser, finishing the longest activity takes 20 minutes, therefore at the moment the maximum number of people that can be processed in one hour is three. However, the longest activity is waiting, therefore this indicates that the appointments system is one area for improvement. The activity that takes the next longest amount of time is cutting hair and up to four people can be processed by one stylist in one hour. If demand is greater than four haircuts per hour, the number of stylists will need to be increased. An increase in the number of stylists may be needed only on the busiest days, for example Friday and Saturday.

The first three steps give a description of the procedure for drawing up a process flow chart and step four provides some indication of the types of issues looked at if improvement is sought.

Operations management should aim for fewer operations and shorter times, while still ensuring that each operation gives the output required by the customer. If bottlenecks occur, the process and/or equipment need to be adjusted so that the process improves.

...

Inventory management

All organisations have to use raw materials, components and/or consumables to carry out their operations and meet forecast demand. Insurance companies and council offices use consumables such as paper, pens, computer discs and stock enough to ensure they do not run out of these items. In contrast, a shoe shop such as Clarks will hold stocks of finished goods in the form of pairs of men's, women's and children's shoes in different styles and sizes. Equally, organisations in the manufacturing sector hold inventory or stock of different types of items. The inventory can be raw materials, for example paper pulp, wheat, coal and crude oil. Inventory can also be components, for example a car production plant will buy in certain items of inventory in component form, such as tyres, lights and assorted engine parts.

...

Materials requirement planning

The dependent demand inventory system can be managed by use of materials requirement planning (MRP). MRP relies on production plans to propose a timetable for when materials orders are required. Consequently the resulting stocks of materials depend directly on a known demand. The alternative is an independent demand inventory system, which means that large enough stocks of materials to cover any probably demand are held.

...

Just in time

... Independent demand inventory systems manage the mismatch by ensuring that stocks are high enough to cover any expected demand. In comparison, dependent demand inventory systems using MRP overcome the stock mismatch by using a master schedule to match the supply of materials approximately to demand. The closer the match of supply to demand, the lower the stock levels needed to cover any mismatches. The just-in-time (JIT) system takes things a stage further and attempts to eliminate the stock mismatch altogether. A just-in-time system is organised so that stock arrives just as it is needed. Accordingly, the immediate nature of JIT systems depends on suppliers and customers working together to achieve the common objective of supplies arriving on time.

...

Quality

Quality can be defined as the ability of a product or service to meet and preferably exceed customer expectations. For example, a breathable hill-walking jacket that keeps out the rain and wind and makes the wearer comfortable fulfils its quality expectation, as does a meal in a restaurant to celebrate your birthday if good food, wine and ambience are in evidence. This illustrates the importance of quality. Quality contributes to helping an organisation remain competitive by producing goods and services of the quality demanded by customers. If the quality fails to meet the quality needs and wants of customers, market share and profits will be lost. Hence managers and organisations invest significant effort into quality management, which is concerned with all aspects of product or service quality.

...

The quality of an organisation's products or services can be viewed from two basic points, inside and outside the organisation. The inside or organisational viewpoint of quality is that the performance of a product or service meets its design specifications exactly. The external or customer viewpoint is defined as how well a product or service does the job for which it was purchased ...

Quality costs

The management of quality will both incur and save costs for an organisation. Suppose that a faulty computer games system is sold to a customer buying a Christmas present for their child. The customer complains and the manufacturer arranges for the system to be repaired. However, money could have been saved if the manufacturer had found the fault prior to the games system leaving the factory, and even more money could have been saved by producing a games system that was fault free in the first instance. These costs are known as external failure costs.

There are three other categories of costs associated with quality: design costs, appraisal costs and internal failure costs. Design costs cover the expense of designing a good-quality product. This involves employing appropriate design staff, considering the type and cost of materials, the number of components, the manufacturing time, the ease of production, the amount of automation used, and the skill level required by the workforce. Appraisal costs cover verifying that the designed quality is the same as the achieved quality, which includes quality control costs such as those for sampling and inspecting the goods and work in progress. Finally, internal failure costs cover the cost of any items not meeting the designed quality. This can cover scrapping the item or returning it to an earlier point in the process to be reworked. There is also the cost of the work carried out on the defective item before it was detected. Therefore, defects should ideally be found as early as possible in the process.

...

Scheduling

Scheduling involves drawing up a timetable of work that will ensure that customer needs and wants are met. Scheduling is critical in making certain that the utilisation of labour and equipment is optimal and that bottlenecks in the process are avoided. Scheduling generally deals with activities that are normally repetitive and short term in nature. Examples of timetables or schedules are shown in Table R4.1.

Table R4.1 Examples of schedules

Railways: Railway timetables for trains, drivers, guards, ticket inspectors, catering staff and passengers
Hospitals: Hospital schedules for operations, patients, nurses, surgeons, beds and operating theatres
Chocolate manufacturer: Chocolate manufacturer producing handmade chocolates has a schedule for customer orders, employees, equipment, raw materials delivery (cocoa, butter, cream and flavourings) and delivery of completed orders

Scheduling aims to meet the master production schedule and achieve low costs and high utilisation of equipment. This may appear to be straightforward and easy, but schedules must take account of many different factors. Take the example of drawing up timetables for first-year university students. The availability and requirements of staff, students, subjects and rooms all have to be balanced. The availability of staff and students has to be considered, for instance, as they can be in only one class at a time, and rooms of the right size and type have to be allocated to a subject at a time when both staff member and students can attend. This will be difficult if the number of rooms is limited or if special facilities such as a computer lab, language lab or science lab are required for the class.

...

Purchasing

The purchasing activity for organisations can be centralised, decentralised or a combination of both.

Centralised purchasing

Centralised purchasing is when the procurement of all purchased items for the whole organisation is arranged and controlled via one department. This allows bulk buying, which usually means that better prices and service can be obtained from suppliers ... Centralised purchasing also yields a consistent standard and quality of purchased products for the whole organisation, reduced administrative costs, streamlined relations with suppliers, and a reduction in transport costs, since orders are delivered in larger quantities.

Decentralised purchasing

Decentralised purchasing occurs when every division or department of the organisation makes its own purchasing decisions, which is less bureaucratic than a centralised purchasing system. In addition, if the divisions or departments of a large organisation are buying from local suppliers who are responsive to their individual needs, it may be more cost effective than centralised purchasing.

Combination of purchasing functions

If neither a centralised nor a decentralised purchasing system is completely appropriate for the organisation, a combination of centralised and decentralised purchasing may be more suitable. If a combination of systems is used, responsibility for certain items, often of a relatively low value, rests with the decentralised system, which is managed by the division or department. In contrast, the centralised part of the system is used for relatively expensive items and infrequent purchases, such as capital expenditure, which may have to be approved by the board of directors.

Distribution

Distribution is concerned with moving finished goods from the manufacturer to customers. A normal distribution system involves finished goods being moved from the manufacturer's premises to the distributor's warehouse until they are allocated to customers. This type of distribution system allows manufacturers to achieve economies of scale by concentrating operations in central locations, which in turn means that distribution costs are reduced as large orders are moved from manufacturer to wholesaler, rather than small orders being moved directly to retailers or consumers.

This also means that the manufacturer does not need to keep large stocks of finished goods. Wholesalers placing large orders with manufacturers will negotiate a reduced unit price and will also stock a range of goods from many suppliers, hence allowing the retailers a choice of goods. If wholesalers offer short lead times and reliable delivery in addition to a good range of stock, retailers can carry less stock and still offer the consumer a wide range of goods.

...

Maintenance

Maintenance activity supports the operations management department by helping ensure that its equipment and facilities are kept in working order. Therefore an organisation's policy on maintenance is integrated with operations policy. This is important as any unplanned shutdown can have a significant effect on production systems, particularly if other carefully planned systems also support operations, such as a JIT inventory management system, as discussed earlier ...

Maintenance has two key aims: to reduce both the frequency and impact of failures. The frequency of failure can be reduced by proper installation of the correct equipment along with a programme of preventive maintenance and replacement of items that are wearing out. The impact of maintenance can be lessened by its being planned for quiet times and/or minimising downtime and repair times.

There are two types of maintenance policy: run to breakdown and preventive maintenance. If the consequences of failure are limited and the equipment is easily replaceable, run to breakdown is the sensible option. There are two ways to respond to a breakdown: emergency action if the breakdown has serious effects, or corrective action at a point in the future if the impact is limited.

Preventive maintenance is carried out on a planned basis. The intervals between maintenance work are established by experience, manufacturers or external authorities. Inspection is an important part of maintenance, especially for items that are expensive to replace or repair.

...

(Source: Capon, C., 2004, *Understanding Organisational Context: Inside and Outside Organisations*, 2nd edn, Harlow, Prentice Hall Financial Times, pp. 153–84.)

Acknowledgements

Grateful acknowledgement is made to the following sources for permission to reproduce material in this book:

Text

Example 2.2: Taylor, P., 'US airlines: Big carriers unlikely to find much relief', *The Financial Times*, January 30, 2003, reprinted with permission; *Example 3.1*: Kelso, P., 'Football: Burns urges radical reforms', *Guardian*, June 11, 2005, Copyright Guardian Newpapers Limited 2005; *Session 4, p.41*: Hofstede, G. (1980) *Culture's Consequences: International Differences in Work Related Values*, London, Sage; *Example 4.1*: Crace, J., 'Feel at home with a job abroad', *Guardian*, October 14, 2000, reprinted with permission from the author; *Example 7.1*: Gascoigne, C., 'Relative advantages of a personal passion' in Capon, C. (2004) *Understanding Organisational Context: Inside and Outside Organisations*, Pearson Education Limited. Reproduced with permission from the author; *Example 7.2*: Adler, C., 'Office Hours: Are you reliant on the family business' *Guardian*, April 11, 2005. Reproduced with permission from the author; *Essential Readings 1, 2 and 3*: Capon, C. (2004) *Understanding Organisational Context Inside and Outside Organisations*, Pearson Education Limited © Pearson Education Limited 2000, 2004.

Tables

Table 2.2: Capon, C. (2004) *Understanding Organisational Context: Inside and Outside Organisations*, Pearson Education Ltd.

Photographs/Illustrations

Page 8: © Philip Wolmuth/reportdigital.co.uk; *Page 12 and 18*: © Mike Baldwin/CartoonStock Ltd; *Page 14*: © Joanne O'Brien/ reportdigital.co.uk; *Page 35*: © Paul Box/reportdigital.co.uk; *Page 36 and 50*: © John Morris/CartoonStock Ltd; *Page 44, 45 and 62:* Ted Goff; *Page 54, 60, 65*: © Randy Glasbergen; *Page 70*: © Empics.

Cover

© Flat Earth/Fotosearch Photography and Stock Footage.

Module team

B120 team

Dr Anja Schaefer
Dr Nik Winchester
Dr Warren Smith
Dr Vira Krakhmal
Barry Jones, *Curriculum Manager*
Carey Stephens
Susan Hughes
Rosie McGookin
Val O'Connor, *Curriculum Assistant*

The original course team

Dr Diane Preston, *Course Team Chair*
Patricia McCarthy, *Course Manager*
Dr Kirstie Ball
Penny Marrington
Fran Myers
Dr Anja Schaefer
Dr George Watson
Rita Gregory, *Course Team Assistant*
Val O'Connor, *Course Team Assistant*

Other contributors

Dr Lorna J. Eller
Mick Fryer
Jonathan Winship

External examiner

Kate Greenan, *Professor of Management Education and Head of School of Accounting, Ulster University*

Developmental testers

Linda Fisher
Adam Messer
John Messer
Marina Ramtohul

Critical readers

Patricia Coffey, *Senior Lecturer, University of Brighton Business School*
Clare Cromarty, *OUBS Associate Lecturer*
Patricia Dawson, *Principal Lecturer, Thames Valley University, retired*
Helen Higson, *Director of Undergraduate Studies, Aston Business School*

Beverly Leeds, *Principal Lecturer, University of Central Lancashire*
Jill Mordaunt, *OUBS Senior Lecturer*
Nigel Walton, *OUBS Associate Lecturer*

Production team

Martin Brazier, *Graphic Designer*
Angela Davies, *Media Assistant*
Richard Dobson, *Editor*
Hannah Eiseman-Renyard, *Editor*
Diane Hopwood, *Rights Assistant*
Lee Johnson, *Media Project Manager*
Siggy Martin, *Assistant Print Buyer*
Katy Nyaaba, *Media Assistant*
Jill Somerscales, *Editor*

The original production team

Holly Clements, *Media Assistant*
Lene Connolly, *Print Buyer*
Jonathan Davies, *Graphic Designer*
Julie Fletcher, *Media Project Manager*
Fiona Harris, *Editor*
Diane Hopwood, *Compositor*
Kate Hunter, *Editor*
Jon Owen, *Graphic Artist*
Deana Plummer, *Picture Researcher*
Diana Russell, *Proofreader*
Dave Richings, *Assistant Print Buyer*
Jill Somerscales, *Editor*